NEXT

When the Clock Strikes:
Faith, Power, and Hope in the End Times

BY LAURAINE WHITE

MISSION STATEMENT

We exist to educate, motivate, and inspire those seeking to know God in a deeper way. We help those seekers to build a relationship with Jesus that goes beyond church attendance, singing in a choir or serving on a church board. Furthermore, we establish with seekers of divine knowledge understanding their identity in Christ, who their enemy is, and how to endure the battles of life. This is accomplished by orchestrating tried and true life strategies that involve prayer, fasting, and the greater works being firmly rooted in them. We believe that miracles, signs and wonders follow us because Jesus's spirit lives in us; therefore, the greater works are done through us.

MIRACLE-MOVEMENT.COM

NEXT

FORWARD

Lauraine

MEET YOUR INSTRUCTOR

Author of:

- Chosen
- The Way Out
- Bulletproof
- A Daughter of the Confederacy
- and many more titles to come!

She is an entrepreneur, real estate broker, former pastor, and lover of Jesus. She's also the mother of three children. loves to sing, cook and travel.

Contact me at:
lwhite@miracle-movement.com

FORWARD

This book was not written casually or conceived in speculation. It was written in obedience. On January 1, 2015, the Lord instructed me to shut in and write over the weekend. What followed was not discipline of intellect alone, but submission of my will. From January 2 through January 4, I remained at my desk, compelled by the Holy Spirit to complete the work set before me. In that single weekend, more than 70,000 words were written—eventually forming three distinct books and the outline for 2 more. That outcome was not human productivity; it was divine urgency.

I have returned repeatedly to that same place of calling since then, yet not without resistance. Distraction, fatigue, and an uncharacteristic inability to focus pressed in on me. Even circumstances seemed to conspire against stillness. Severe weather marked every weekend in January 2026 in Georgia, as if creation itself was calling for pause. Yet responsibilities—particularly my service in corporate worship—competed for that time. Still, I came to understand this truth clearly: God will not be denied what He has assigned.

The enemy does not want the people of God to understand the times and seasons. Scripture, however, tells us plainly that God does.

From the beginning, the Lord has spoken through His prophets to prepare His people for what comes next—not to terrify them, but to anchor them. Jesus Himself warned repeatedly of what would precede His return, not to produce fear, but faithfulness. He desires a people with lamps burning and oil in reserve, ready to endure until the end. That oil is the precious Holy Spirit, given not only to seal our salvation, but to guide us into all truth.

I have studied the end times for over twenty years, with particular intensity in the last three. This book emerges from that long obedience—grounded in Scripture, tested by prayer, and constrained by reverence.

5

NEXT

Accordingly, this work approaches the subject of the end times with biblical seriousness, prophetic sobriety, and pastoral responsibility. I do not claim secret knowledge, hidden timelines, or exclusive revelation. I reject fear-driven eschatology, date-setting, and sensational speculation that distract believers from holiness, endurance, and obedience. Likewise, I reject theological frameworks that spiritualize away Christ's return, minimize suffering, or mute Jesus's explicit warnings in the name of comfort or intellectual convenience.

This work is rooted in the conviction that Scripture interprets Scripture; that Jesus meant what He said, and that the prophetic words spoken by Christ and the apostles were given to prepare—not confuse or frighten—the Church.

This work declares without hesitation:

- The visible, bodily return of Jesus Christ
- A future time of unprecedented tribulation
- The resurrection of the dead
- The gathering of the elect
- The ultimate defeat of evil
- The restoration of all things under Christ's reign

I engage historic and biblically sound thought as a faithful framework for understanding the sequence and gravity of end-time events, while remaining cautious where Scripture allows mystery. I acknowledge partial historical fulfillments of prophecy without denying a future, global consummation. I resist systems that remove the Church from suffering prematurely or strip prophecy of its literal and moral force.

Above all, this book is Christ-centered. The end times are not primarily about Antichrists, calamities, or collapse. They are about the revealing of the King, the purification of His people, and the vindication of righteousness.

NEXT does not call readers to escape the world, but to stand faithfully within it—watching, praying, enduring, and shining—until He returns.

CHAPTER 1
WATCH THE FIG TREE

"Now learn this lesson from the fig tree: As soon as its twigs get tender and its leaves come out, you know that summer is near. Even so, when you see all these things, you know that it is near, right at the door."

MATTHEW 24:32-33 NIV

WATCH THE FIG TREE

Jesus never told His disciples to guess. He told them to watch. But what were they to watch for? It wasn't to watch the sky in panic. It wasn't even to watch the news in obsession or each other in suspicion, but to watch with discernment.

"Learn this lesson from the fig tree," He said. *"As soon as its twigs get tender and its leaves come out, you know that summer is near. Even so, when you see all these things, you know that it is near, right at the door."* [Matt. 24:32-33, NIV]

The fig tree does not shout and does not announce itself with spectacle. It simply responds to the season. And Jesus rebuked an entire generation—not for ignorance of Scripture, but for blindness to timing. They could interpret the weather, predict the skies, read the natural signs—but they could not discern the spiritual hour standing in front of them.

That rebuke still rings true today. The tragedy of the last days will not be that the signs were unclear. It will be that they were ignored, dismissed, or explained away.

We live in a generation that knows everything—yet discerns nothing. A people flooded with information but starved for wisdom. We scroll past birth pains as if they are coincidences, label warnings as hysteria, and treat Jesus's own words as optional metaphors. But Scripture never presents the end times as a puzzle to be solved. It presents them as a season to be recognized.

Wars erupt and are normalized. Nations rage and call it politics. The earth groans and we blame only systems. The truth is betrayed and we call it progress. Love grows cold and we consider it maturity.

NEXT

WATCH THE FIG TREE

And still Jesus says: Watch. Watching is not fear. It's not obsession or speculation. Watching is alignment. It is the posture of a servant who knows the Master will return. It is also the awareness of a bride who keeps her lamp filled. It's the discipline of a people who refuse to be lulled asleep by delay.

The danger of the last days is not chaos—it's complacency. *"Just as it was in the days of Noah,"* Jesus said, *"so also will it be in the days of the Son of Man. People were eating, drinking, marrying and being given in marriage up to the day Noah entered the ark. Then the flood came and destroyed them all. It was the same in the days of Lot. People were eating and drinking, buying and selling, planting and building. But the day Lot left Sodom, fire and sulfur rained down from heaven and destroyed them all."* [Luke 17:26-29, NIV]

They were not warned because they lacked information. They were warned because they lacked discernment. The signs of the times are not given so we can draw charts. They are given so we can examine our hearts. Because the end will not expose what we believe. It will expose what we love.

To watch the fig tree is to admit that history is moving somewhere; that evil has an expiration date, that suffering is not endless, and that Christ is not absent—He is patient. Every generation is tempted to think the warnings apply to someone else and believes delay means denial. But the Scriptures insist: delay is mercy.

The fig tree is speaking. Its leaves are not subtle anymore. The season is not hidden, and ignorance is no longer innocent. The question is not whether the signs are happening but whether we will recognize them without fear, respond without frenzy, and remain faithful without compromise. Because the end does not belong to the fearful. It belongs to the faithful. And those who watch will not be surprised.

NEXT

WATCH THE FIG TREE

KEY SCRIPTURES

Please read the scriptures, then answer the questions that follow.

ONE

MATTHEW 24:32–33 NIV

"Now learn this lesson from the fig tree: As soon as its twigs get tender and its leaves come out, you know that summer is near. Even so, when you see all these things, you know that it is near, right at the door."

TWO

LUKE 12:54–56 NIV

He said to the crowd: "When you see a cloud rising in the west, immediately you say, 'It's going to rain,' and it does. And when the south wind blows, you say, 'It's going to be hot,' and it is. Hypocrites! You know how to interpret the appearance of the earth and the sky. How is it that you don't know how to interpret this present time?"

THREE

1 THESSALONIANS 5:4–6 NIV

"But you, brothers and sisters, are not in darkness so that this day should surprise you like a thief. You are all children of the light and children of the day. We do not belong to the night or to the darkness. So then, let us not be like others, who are asleep, but let us be awake and sober."

FOUR

MATTHEW 24:37–39 NIV

"As it was in the days of Noah, so it will be at the coming of the Son of Man. For in the days before the flood, people were eating and drinking, marrying and giving in marriage, up to the day Noah entered the ark; and they knew nothing about what would happen until the flood came and took them all away. That is how it will be at the coming of the Son of Man."

FIVE

LUKE 17:28–30 NIV

"It was the same in the days of Lot. People were eating and drinking, buying and selling, planting and building. But the day Lot left Sodom, fire and sulfur rained down from heaven and destroyed them all. 'It will be just like this on the day the Son of Man is revealed.'"

KEY SCRIPTURES

Please read the scriptures, then answer the questions that follow.

ONE

2 PETER 3:8-9 NIV

"But do not forget this one thing, dear friends: With the Lord a day is like a thousand years, and a thousand years are like a day. The Lord is not slow in keeping his promise, as some understand slowness. Instead he is patient with you, not wanting anyone to perish, but everyone to come to repentance."

TWO

ROMANS 13:11-12 NIV

"And do this, understanding the present time: The hour has already come for you to wake up from your slumber, because our salvation is nearer now than when we first believed. The night is nearly over; the day is almost here. So let us put aside the deeds of darkness and put on the armor of light."

THREE

HABAKKUK 2:3 NIV

"For the revelation awaits an appointed time; it speaks of the end and will not prove false. Though it linger, wait for it; it will certainly come and will not delay."

FOUR

MATTHEW 25:1-13 NIV

"At that time the kingdom of heaven will be like ten virgins who took their lamps and went out to meet the bridegroom. Five of them were foolish and five were wise. The foolish ones took their lamps but did not take any oil with them. The wise ones, however, took oil in jars along with their lamps. The bridegroom was a long time in coming, and they all became drowsy and fell asleep. At midnight the cry rang out: 'Here's the bridegroom! Come out to meet him!' Then all the virgins woke up and trimmed their lamps. The foolish ones said to the wise, 'Give us some of your oil; our lamps are going out.' 'No,' they replied, 'there may not be enough for both us and you. Instead, go to those who sell oil and buy some for yourselves.' But while they were on their way to buy the oil, the bridegroom arrived. The virgins who were ready went in with him to the wedding banquet. And the door was shut. Later the others also came. 'Lord, Lord,' they said, 'open the door for us!' But he replied, 'Truly I tell you, I don't know you.' Therefore keep watch, because you do not know the day or the hour."

GROUP DISCUSSION QUESTIONS

Consider the scriptures read, then answer the following questions.

What does "watching" look like in daily life without becoming fearful or obsessive?

How do we practically live alert without losing peace?

Where do you see signs being normalized, dismissed, or explained away in our culture?

What current priorities in your life might be exposed by this realization?

How can the Church cultivate discernment instead of distraction in this season?

What practices help keep lamps filled and hearts awake?

NEXT

Prayer

Dear Father,

Forgive us for knowing so much and discerning so
little.
Cleanse us from complacency and distraction.
Give us eyes to see the seasons,
ears to hear Your warnings,
and hearts willing to align without delay.
Teach us to recognize mercy in Your patience
and urgency in Your silence.
By Your Holy Spirit, keep our lamps filled, our love
pure,
and our obedience ready.
We refuse sleep that dulls our awareness.
We reject compromise and choose faithfulness.
We declare that we will not be surprised or fearful.
We will be found watching and ready.
In the name of Jesus our Lord we pray,
Amen.

CHAPTER 2
FALSE
CHRISTS AND
FALSE HOPE

"For false messiahs and
false prophets will
appear and perform
great signs and wonders
to deceive, if possible,
even the elect."

–*Matthew 24:24 NIV*

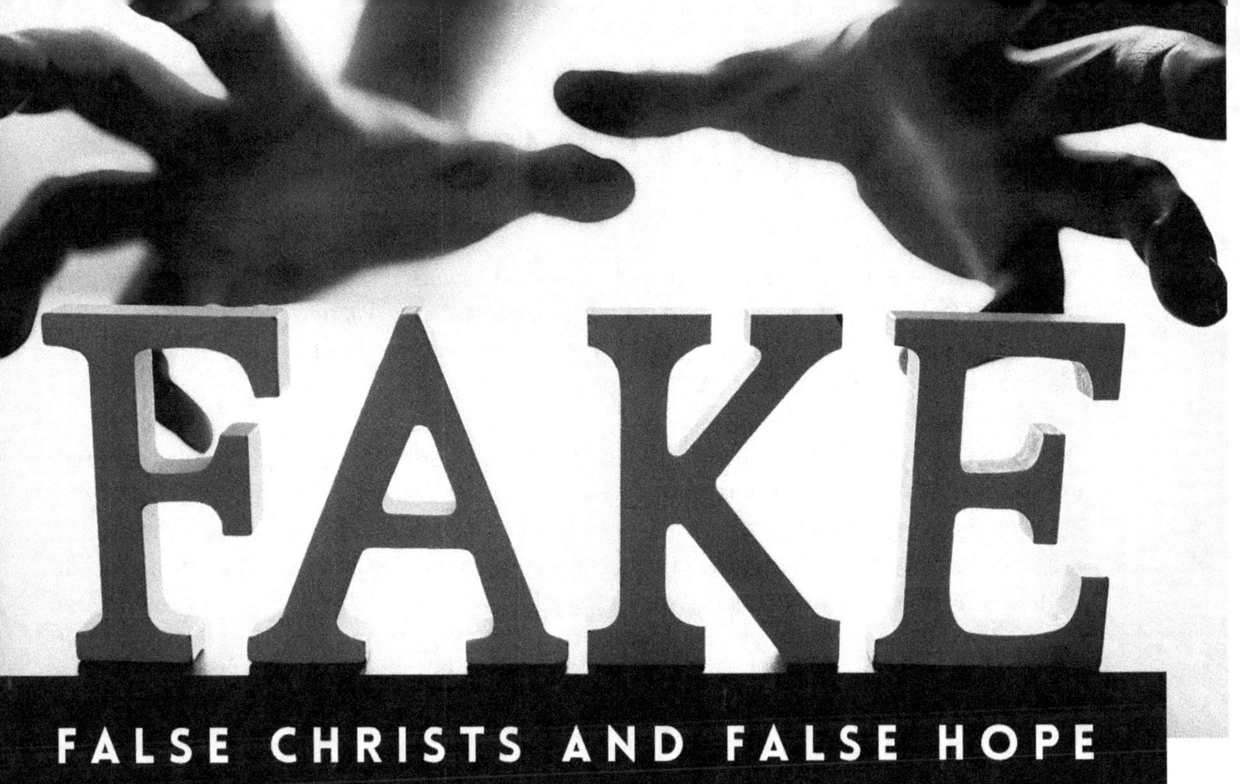

When the disciples came to Jesus privately and asked, *"What will be the sign of Your coming and of the end of the age?"* They were expecting headlines—wars, earthquakes, judgment, and heavenly upheaval. But Jesus did not begin with catastrophe. He began with a command. His first words were not about destruction, but deception: *"Watch out that no one deceives you"* (Matthew 24:4 NIV). That order matters. Before famine, persecution, tribulation, or the shaking of the heavens, Jesus wanted to protect them from those who deceive. Deception comes first. This tells us something unsettling and crucial: the greatest danger of the last days is not chaos—it is convincing lies disguised as truth.

A false Christ is not merely someone who claims to be Jesus. A false Christ is far more subtle and far more dangerous. A false Christ is anything—or anyone—that promises salvation, security, identity, or meaning apart from full submission to the true Christ. False Christs offer peace without repentance, power without holiness, hope without truth, and comfort without the cross. Some will emerge through politics. Some will arise in spiritual language. Some will be ideological, philosophical, or cultural. Some will quote Scripture fluently and speak with authority. Jesus never said they would appear wicked. He warned that they would appear convincing.

False hope does not look like despair. False hope feels confident and comforting. It is assurance placed in the wrong source. It sounds like trusting a system to save us, a leader to fix what is broken, a movement to deliver justice without righteousness, or a version of faith that costs nothing and demands nothing.   False hope thrives in unstable times

17

FALSE CHRISTS AND FALSE HOPE

because fear breeds desperation, and desperation lowers discernment. Scripture warns that in the last days people will trade truth for comfort. *"They will turn their ears away from the truth and turn aside to myths." [2 Tim. 4:4, NIV]* Myths feel safer than repentance. Lies feel merciful when truth demands surrender.

Deception rarely announces itself. It does not arrive wearing darkness; it comes adorned in light. It works through partial truth—just enough accuracy to gain trust. It stirs emotional appeal through fear, outrage, or false compassion. It removes the necessity of repentance while still offering belonging. It creates urgency—act now or be left behind. It flatters the listener by affirming what they already want to believe. Paul warned the church that Satan does not disguise himself as darkness, but as light. *"For Satan himself masquerades as an angel of light" [2 Cor. 11:14, NIV].* Light that does not lead to Christ is still darkness, no matter how warm it feels.

Jesus makes a sobering statement when He says that deception will be so strong it could deceive even the elect—if that were possible. This reveals two uncomfortable truths. First, intelligence alone does not protect believers from deception. Second, end-time deception is aimed at the Church, not the unbelieving world. False Christs are not primarily sent to atheists; they are sent to those who know Scripture but may not fully obey it. Knowledge without submission creates vulnerability. Familiarity with truth does not equal faithfulness to it.

Jesus explicitly warned that false messiahs would perform great signs and wonders. Supernatural power, therefore, is not proof of God's approval. Miracles alone are not validation. Scripture is clear: signs must align with truth, power must submit to Christ, and fruit must reflect holiness. Jesus Himself said, *"Not everyone who says to me, 'Lord, Lord,' will enter the kingdom of heaven, but only the one who does the will of my Father who is in heaven." [Matt. 7:21, NIV].* The ultimate test is not supernatural ability, spiritual experience, or public acclaim. The test is obedience to the will of the Father.

Jesus warned that many would say, "Here is the Christ," or "There He is," and He commanded His followers not to believe it. False Christs thrive in hidden rooms, exclusive revelations, secret knowledge, private teachings, and personality-driven movements that elevate a voice above Scripture. The true return of Christ will not require an announcement, an invitation, or a special insider audience. *"For as lightning comes from the east and flashes to the west, so will be the coming of the Son of Man." [Matt. 24:27, ESV]* There will be no secrecy, no ambiguity, and no confusion.

NEXT

FALSE CHRISTS AND FALSE HOPE

Jesus does not tell His disciples to chase every claim or investigate every voice. He tells them to remain rooted. The antidote to deception is not paranoia—it is devotion to the Savior. It demands a love for truth, endurance in obedience, a deep familiarity with Scripture, and sensitivity to the Holy Spirit. *"And with all wicked deception for those who are perishing, because they refused to love the truth and so be saved." [2 Thessalonians 2:10, ESV]*. Deception loses its power wherever truth is cherished more than comfort.

The last days will not expose who can identify deception in others. They will reveal who has refused it within themselves. The real question is not whether you can spot a false Christ. The real question is this: what are you tempted to trust instead of Christ when pressure comes? False Christs won't replace Jesus outright. They replace dependence on Him and that is why Jesus began here.

FALSE CHRISTS AND FALSE HOPE

KEY SCRIPTURES

Please read the scriptures, then answer the questions that follow.

MATTHEW 24:24 NIV

"For false messiahs and false prophets will appear and perform great signs and wonders to deceive, if possible, even the elect."

MATTHEW 24:4 NIV

Jesus answered: "Watch out that no one deceives you."

2 THESSALONIANS 2:9–10 NIV

"The coming of the lawless one will be in accordance with how Satan works. He will use all sorts of displays of power through signs and wonders that serve the lie, and all the ways that wickedness deceives those who are perishing. They perish because they refused to love the truth and so be saved."

2 CORINTHIANS 11:14 NIV

"And no wonder, for Satan himself masquerades as an angel of light."

2 TIMOTHY 4:3–4 NIV

"For the time will come when people will not put up with sound doctrine. Instead, to suit their own desires, they will gather around them a great number of teachers to say what their itching ears want to hear. They will turn their ears away from the truth and turn aside to myths."

NEXT

FALSE CHRISTS AND FALSE HOPE

KEY SCRIPTURES

Please read the scriptures, then answer the questions that follow.

ONE

MATTHEW 7:21-23 NIV

"Not everyone who says to me, 'Lord, Lord,' will enter the kingdom of heaven, but only the one who does the will of my Father who is in heaven. Many will say to me on that day, 'Lord, Lord, did we not prophesy in your name and in your name drive out demons and in your name perform many miracles?' Then I will tell them plainly, 'I never knew you. Away from me, you evildoers!'"

TWO

MATTHEW 24:26-27 NIV

"So if anyone tells you, 'There he is, out in the wilderness,' do not go out; or, 'Here he is, in the inner rooms,' do not believe it. For as lightning that comes from the east is visible even in the west, so will be the coming of the Son of Man."

THREE

JOHN 14:6 NIV

Jesus answered, "I am the way and the truth and the life. No one comes to the Father except through me."

FOUR

COLOSSIANS 2:8-10 NIV

"See to it that no one takes you captive through hollow and deceptive philosophy, which depends on human tradition and the elemental spiritual forces of this world rather than on Christ. For in Christ all the fullness of the Deity lives in bodily form, and in Christ you have been brought to fullness. He is the head over every power and authority."

FIVE

HOSEA 4:6 NIV

"My people are destroyed from lack of knowledge. 'Because you have rejected knowledge, I also reject you as my priests; because you have ignored the law of your God, I also will ignore your children.'"

NEXT

GROUP DISCUSSION QUESTIONS

Consider the scriptures read, then answer the following questions.

How does Jesus describe deception in the last days and where do you see false hope operating today?

Why do you think Jesus prioritized deception over destruction in His end-times teaching?

What are modern examples of "false Christs" that promise salvation or security apart from Christ?

Why are signs, wonders, and spiritual experiences insufficient tests of truth?

What comforts are you personally tempted to trust when pressure or fear increases?

What helps you test spiritual messages wisely?

NEXT

Lord Jesus,
Expose every counterfeit competing for our trust and
loyalty, every substitute we have leaned on, and
every voice we have followed other than yours.
Give us a love for truth that costs us something.
Root us so deeply in You that no false Christ can move
us.
Train our eyes to see beyond signs,
our hearts to resist comfort that does not lead to the
cross,
and our lives to reflect obedience to the Father.
We choose devotion over distraction,
submission over sensation,
and Christ over every substitute.
Keep us faithful when the pressures of the last days
weigh in on us as we surrender our lives to you.
In Your holy name we pray,
Amen.

CHAPTER 3
A WORLD AT WAR

"You will hear of wars and rumors of wars but see to it that you are not alarmed. Such things must happen, but the end is still to come."

—MATTHEW 24:6 NIV

A WORLD AT WAR

"You will hear of wars and rumors of wars but see to it that you are not alarmed. Such things must happen, but the end is still to come."
—Matthew 24:6 NIV

If war has marked human history since its beginning, why did Jesus include it as a sign of the last days? Because in the end, war does not merely continue—it intensifies, multiplies, and converges. Jesus does not present war as the end itself, but as evidence that something deeper is unraveling beneath the surface of the world. And yet, in the same breath that He acknowledges conflict, He issues an unexpected command: *"See that you are not alarmed."* This is not denial of reality. It is discernment in the face of it.

Jesus compresses three critical truths into His warning. First, wars will happen. Second, they will increase in frequency and scale. Third, they are not the final signal of the end. *"Nation will rise against nation, and kingdom against kingdom."* [Matt. 24:7 NIV] This language points beyond isolated conflicts and local disputes. It describes systemic instability—alliances fracturing, power structures shifting, and long-standing balances collapsing. War becomes a global language, spoken across borders and broadcast into every home.

Scripture consistently links the escalation of war with the inner condition of humanity and the moral posture of nations. Pride, competition for dominance, economic pressure, moral collapse, and spiritual rebellion all converge to produce conflict. James confronts this reality with piercing clarity: *"What causes fights and quarrels among you? Don't they come from your desires that battle within you? You desire but do not have, so you kill. You covet but you cannot get what you want, so you quarrel and fight. You do not have because you do not ask God. When you ask, you do not receive, because you ask with wrong motives, that you may spend what you get on your pleasures. You adulterous people, don't you know that friendship with the world means enmity against God? Therefore, anyone who chooses to be a friend of the world becomes an enemy of God."* [James 4:1-4, NIV]

External wars are the overflow of internal disorder. As restraint weakens—politically, morally, and spiritually—conflict accelerates and spreads. Jesus does not only warn of wars, but of rumors of wars.

NEXT

This detail is deliberate. Fear itself becomes a weapon in the last days. Rumors destabilize economies, justify authoritarian control, inflame panic, nationalism, and condition populations to accept emergency measures without question. The end times are marked not only by conflict, but by the constant expectation of conflict. A world perpetually on edge is a world easier to manipulate.

Jesus does not say ideology against ideology or army against army. He says nation against nation. This signals the breakdown of international trust, the fracturing of treaties, the resurgence of nationalism, and the transformation of identity into a battleground. Even within nations, internal divisions mirror the same spirit of hostility and fragmentation. Jesus is describing a world that has lost its ability—and often its desire—to cooperate.

This is why believers are explicitly commanded not to panic. Fear clouds judgment. When fear takes hold, discernment collapses, hope shrinks into survivalism, witness is compromised, and allegiance becomes negotiable. Jesus does not deny danger, but He forbids hysteria. Fear makes people willing to trade truth for protection, conviction for comfort, and obedience for safety.

War, then, is a sign—but it is not a signal to hide. The early Church lived under constant threat of Roman occupation, political violence, persecution, and execution. Yet they were never instructed to retreat from faithfulness. Jesus told them plainly, "When you hear of wars and uprisings, do not be frightened. These things must happen first, but the end will not come right away." [Luke 21:9, NIV] War exposes whether faith is rooted in Christ or anchored in stability. When peace disappears, foundations are revealed.

A believer's proper posture embraces tension without twisting the truth. It recognizes prophetic significance without glorifying conflict, without rooting for collapse, and without demonizing entire peoples. War is tragic and sobering. It is not entertainment or prophetic theater. Even as Jesus prophesied judgment, He wept over cities. Grief and truth were never separated in Him.

A WORLD AT WAR

Wars reveal what nations truly worship. They expose how quickly morality bends under pressure, whose lives are deemed expendable, and whether peace was genuine or merely convenient. They uncover the illusion that human systems can save us. What appears solid in times of peace often proves fragile under fire.

In a world at war, the Church is not called to panic or propagandize. It is called to pray for leaders, to care for the vulnerable, to refuse hatred, to speak truth without allegiance to violence, and to remember that Christ's kingdom is not of this world. Jesus said it plainly: *"My kingdom is not of this world. If it were, my servants would fight to prevent my arrest by the Jewish leaders. But now my kingdom is from another place."* [John 18:36, NIV]

Jesus tells us that wars must happen—but they are not yet the end. The danger is not that we believe the end is near. The danger is that believers will stop watching once war becomes normal. War is not the conclusion. It is the shaking that asks a final, searching question: when peace disappears, where is your confidence truly anchored?

A WORLD AT WAR

KEY SCRIPTURES

Please read the scriptures, then answer the questions that follow.

ONE

MATTHEW 24:6-7 NIV

"You will hear of wars and rumors of wars, but see to it that you are not alarmed. Such things must happen, but the end is still to come. Nation will rise against nation, and kingdom against kingdom. There will be famines and earthquakes in various places."

TWO

LUKE 21:9 NIV

"When you hear of wars and uprisings, do not be frightened. These things must happen first, but the end will not come right away."

THREE

JAMES 4:1-3 NIV

"What causes fights and quarrels among you? Don't they come from your desires that battle within you? You desire but do not have, so you kill. You covet but you cannot get what you want, so you quarrel and fight. You do not have because you do not ask God. When you ask, you do not receive, because you ask with wrong motives, that you may spend what you get on your pleasures."

FOUR

PSALM 46:1-3 NIV

"God is our refuge and strength, an ever-present help in trouble. Therefore we will not fear, though the earth give way and the mountains fall into the heart of the sea, though its waters roar and foam and the mountains quake with their surging."

FIVE

PSALM 46:6-10 NIV

"Nations are in uproar, kingdoms fall; he lifts his voice, the earth melts. The Lord Almighty is with us; the God of Jacob is our fortress. Come and see what the Lord has done, the desolations he has brought on the earth. He makes wars cease to the ends of the earth. He breaks the bow and shatters the spear; he burns the shields with fire. He says, 'Be still, and know that I am God; I will be exalted among the nations, I will be exalted in the earth.'"

NEXT

KEY SCRIPTURES

Please read the scriptures, then answer the questions that follow.

ONE

ISAIAH 2:4 NIV

"He will judge between the nations and will settle disputes for many peoples. They will beat their swords into plowshares and their spears into pruning hooks. Nation will not take up sword against nation, nor will they train for war anymore."

TWO

JOHN 18:36 NIV

"Jesus said, 'My kingdom is not of this world. If it were, my servants would fight to prevent my arrest by the Jewish leaders. But now my kingdom is from another place.'"

THREE

ROMANS 12:19–21 NIV

"Do not take revenge, my dear friends, but leave room for God's wrath, for it is written: 'It is mine to avenge; I will repay,' says the Lord. On the contrary: 'If your enemy is hungry, feed him; if he is thirsty, give him something to drink. In doing this, you will heap burning coals on his head.' Do not be overcome by evil, but overcome evil with good.'"

FOUR

1 TIMOTHY 2:1–4 NIV

"I urge, then, first of all, that petitions, prayers, intercession and thanksgiving be made for all people—for kings and all those in authority, that we may live peaceful and quiet lives in all godliness and holiness. This is good, and pleases God our Savior, who wants all people to be saved and to come to a knowledge of the truth."

FIVE

HEBREWS 12:26–28 NIV

"At that time his voice shook the earth, but now he has promised, 'Once more I will shake not only the earth but also the heavens.' The words 'once more' indicate the removing of what can be shaken—that is, created things—so that what cannot be shaken may remain. Therefore, since we are receiving a kingdom that cannot be shaken, let us be thankful, and so worship God acceptably with reverence and awe."

NEXT

GROUP DISCUSSION QUESTIONS

Consider the scriptures read, then answer the following questions.

How do wars affect your sense of security and What does fear threaten to distort in our faith?

How do "rumors of wars" function differently than wars themselves?

Where do you see fear being used as a tool today?

What does war reveal about what nations and individuals really worship?

How can the Church remain compassionate and truthful without becoming partisan or violent in a world at war?

Jesus told us to not be alarmed. What helps you remain spiritually grounded during global crises?

31

Dear Heavenly Father,
Guard our hearts from panic and hatred.
Keep us from confusing violence with power
or collapse with Your kingdom.
Teach us to stand firm when the world shakes,
to love when nations rage,
and to trust You when peace disappears.
Expose false foundations
and anchor us in what cannot be shaken.
We decree that we will remain faithful witnesses in
a world at war, until the day Your true peace
reigns.
In the holy name of Jesus we pray,
Amen.

CHAPTER 4 CREATION GROANS

"For the creation waits in eager expectation for the children of God to be revealed. For the creation was subjected to frustration, not by its own choice, but by the will of the one who subjected it, in hope that the creation itself will be liberated from its bondage to decay and brought into the freedom and glory of the children of God. We know that the whole creation has been groaning as in the pains of childbirth right up to the present time. Not only so, but we ourselves, who have the firstfruits of the Spirit, groan inwardly as we wait eagerly for our adoption to sonship, the redemption of our bodies."

Romans 8:19-23 NIV

CREATION GROANS

Jesus deliberately included creation in His warnings about the last days. Earthquakes, famines, and natural upheaval are often misunderstood—either dismissed as coincidence or weaponized as proof of God's punishment. Jesus does neither. Instead, He frames these events as birth pains. *"All these are the beginning of birth pains."* [Matt. 24:8, NIV] Birth pains are not random. They are purposeful, progressive, and irreversible. They signal that something new is coming into being, not merely that something old is breaking apart.

Creation is not silent in this process. The apostle Paul reveals a staggering truth: *"We know that the whole creation has been groaning as in the pains of childbirth right up to the present time."* [Rom. 8:22, NIV] Creation groans because it has been subjected to frustration—not by its own choice, but through human rebellion. Sin did not only fracture humanity; it disrupted the created order itself. The earth is responding to a spiritual condition. What we see shaking in nature reflects what has long been disordered in the moral and spiritual realms.

Earthquakes represent more than geological movement. Throughout Scripture, shaking signals divine intervention, the removal of false security, and the exposure of fragile foundations. God declares, *"At that time his voice shook the earth, but now he has promised, 'Once more I will shake not only the earth but also the heavens."* [Hebrews 12:26, NIV] Shaking reveals what can endure. The question is not why the earth is shaking; the question is what are we standing on when it does.

NEXT

CREATION GROANS

"For the creation waits in eager expectation for the children of God to be revealed." (Romans 8:19 NIV)

Famines expose scarcity in a world that is often marked by excess. They are not always caused by the absence of resources, but by mismanagement, injustice, and greed. History consistently links famine with the oppression of the poor, the hoarding of provision, and the corruption of leadership. The prophet Joel cried out over ruined fields and devastated land, revealing a people treated as expendable. [Joel 1] Famines strip away polite narratives and confront societies with a brutal question: when resources grow scarce, who eats first?

Jesus says these events will occur "in various places." They will not be isolated, rare, or hidden. Creation itself becomes a witness. Just as the heavens declared the glory of God in the beginning, they will declare His approaching intervention at the end. The created order testifies that history is moving toward a decisive moment.

These signs are not permission to assign blame or invitation to mock superiority, or tools for fear-mongering. Jesus never celebrates calamity—He interprets it. He teaches His followers how to see rightly without becoming cruel, detached, or sensational.

When creation groans, believers are not called to commentary but to compassion. The faithful are called to pray instead of speculate. When the earth shakes, believers should not become indifferent but are called to action on behalf of the vulnerable. Jesus says, *"When these things begin to take place, stand up and lift up your heads, because your redemption is drawing near."* [Luke 21:28, NIV] Groaning always precedes glory. Pain gives way to promise.

There is a deeper warning embedded in these signs. If the Church ignores the groaning of creation, it risks becoming detached from reality and if it explains away every sign, it risks missing the moment. Creation is not panicking. It is responding and Jesus's instruction is clear: *pay attention.*

CREATION GROANS

KEY SCRIPTURES

Please read the scriptures, then answer the questions that follow.

ROMANS 8:22-23 NIV

"We know that the whole creation has been groaning as in the pains of childbirth right up to the present time. Not only so, but we ourselves, who have the firstfruits of the Spirit, groan inwardly as we wait eagerly for our adoption to sonship, the redemption of our bodies."

MATTHEW 24:8 NIV

"All these are the beginning of birth pains."

ROMANS 8:19-21 NIV

"For the creation waits in eager expectation for the children of God to be revealed. For the creation was subjected to frustration, not by its own choice, but by the will of the one who subjected it, in hope that the creation itself will be liberated from its bondage to decay and brought into the freedom and glory of the children of God."

HEBREWS 12:26-28 NIV

"At that time his voice shook the earth, but now he has promised, 'Once more I will shake not only the earth but also the heavens.' The words 'once more' indicate the removing of what can be shaken—that is, created things —so that what cannot be shaken may remain. Therefore, since we are receiving a kingdom that cannot be shaken, let us be thankful, and so worship God acceptably with reverence and awe."

HAGGAI 2:6-7 NIV

"This is what the Lord Almighty says: 'In a little while I will once more shake the heavens and the earth, the sea and the dry land. I will shake all nations, and what is desired by all nations will come, and I will fill this house with glory,' says the Lord Almighty."

NEXT

CREATION GROANS

KEY SCRIPTURES

Please read the scriptures, then answer the questions that follow.

JOEL 1:15 NIV (READ ENTIRE CHAPTER)

"Alas for that day! For the day of the Lord is near; it will come like destruction from the Almighty."

PSALM 46:2-3 NIV

"Therefore we will not fear, though the earth give way and the mountains fall into the heart of the sea, though its waters roar and foam and the mountains quake with their surging."

ISAIAH 24:5-6 NIV

"The earth is defiled by its people; they have disobeyed the laws, violated the statutes and broken the everlasting covenant. Therefore a curse consumes the earth; its people must bear their guilt. Therefore earth's inhabitants are burned up, and very few are left."

REVELATION 11:18 NIV

"The nations were angry, and your wrath has come. The time has come for judging the dead, and for rewarding your servants the prophets and your people who revere your name, both great and small—and for destroying those who destroy the earth."

LUKE 21:28 NIV

"When these things begin to take place, stand up and lift up your heads, because your redemption is drawing near."

NEXT

GROUP DISCUSSION QUESTIONS

Consider the scriptures read, then answer the following questions.

Why does Jesus describe natural upheaval as "birth pains" rather than punishment?

How does understanding this truth reframe how we interpret suffering?

What does the groaning of creation reveal about humanity's spiritual and moral condition?

How do famines expose societal values and priorities?

What does scarcity reveal about who is protected and who is expendable?

What does it mean to respond with compassion instead of commentary when disaster strikes?

NEXT

Creator and Redeemer,
Give us eyes to see without fear,
hearts that grieve without hardness,
and faith that stands firm when the earth shakes.
Expose false foundations
and root us in what cannot be moved.
Teach us to respond to groaning with
compassion,
to shaking with trust,
and to pain with hope.
As creation cries out,
keep us steady, attentive, faithful,
and ready for the glory to come.
In the name of Jesus we pray,
Amen.

CHAPTER 5
PESTILENCE, DISEASE, AND GLOBAL FRAGILITY

"There will be great earthquakes, famines, and pestilences in various places, and fearful events and great signs from heaven."

—Luke 21:11 NIV

PESTILENCE, DISEASE, AND GLOBAL FRAGILITY

Jesus did not speak of disease as a metaphor. He was very clear that widespread disease would come. Pestilence is not merely sickness; it is the rapid spread of vulnerability across borders, bodies, and bureaucracies once thought secure. In the last days, disease does not remain local. It travels. It multiplies. It exposes how interconnected and fragile the world has become. What once seemed distant arrives at the doorstep. What was assumed to be controlled proves otherwise.

COVID-19 exposed how interconnected and fragile the modern world has become. A microscopic virus halted economies, overwhelmed hospitals, emptied sanctuaries, and silenced stadiums. Supply chains became fractured. Borders closed. Schools shut their doors. The illusion of uninterrupted progress dissolved almost overnight. Humanity discovered that efficiency without resilience is vulnerability.

Scripture is not silent about such moments. Throughout the Old Testament, pestilence often accompanied exposure—not arbitrary cruelty, but revelation.

43

PESTILENCE, DISEASE, AND GLOBAL FRAGILITY

In Numbers 12:1–15, Miriam's leprosy exposed rebellion that had already taken root. What was whispered in private became visible in public because God removed its cover. Pride was revealed and repentance was required. The camp had to stop moving until restoration occurred.

In 2 Samuel 24:10–25, after David placed confidence in military numbers by taking a census rather than in God, a plague swept through Israel. Seventy thousand people fell dead. The pestilence revealed misplaced trust. David confessed his sin against God's order, built an altar, and sought mercy. The crisis uncovered a deeper spiritual condition.

In 2 Chronicles 7:13–14, God speaks directly: "When I shut up the heavens so that there is no rain, or command locusts to devour the land, or send a plague among my people, if my people who are called by my name humble themselves and pray… then I will hear from heaven." The plague is not meaningless. It becomes an invitation to humility.

COVID-19 functioned in similar ways. It revealed the illusion that humans are the masters of its own destinies. Modern society prides itself on medicine, technology, and progress, yet disease reminds us how quickly confidence collapses. A microscopic agent can halt economies, overwhelm hospitals, disrupt supply chains, and isolate entire populations. Scripture is not dismissive of human

NEXT

CHAPTER FIVE

PESTILENCE, DISEASE, AND GLOBAL FRAGILITY

"There will be great earthquakes, famines, and pestilences in various places, and fearful events and great signs from heaven."
—Luke 21:11 NIV

advancement, but it is honest about human limits. Pestilence humbles the proud and interrupts the myth that humanity is self-sustaining.

Throughout Scripture, disease often accompanies moments of moral reckoning—not as arbitrary punishment, but as exposure. It reveals inequalities long ignored, systems already strained, and priorities that are misaligned. Who receives care first? Who is protected? Who is left behind? Disease uncovers the fault lines of justice and compassion. It shows whether societies value human life universally or selectively.

Jesus's warning includes "fearful events." Pestilence carries psychological weight as much as physical harm. Fear spreads faster than illness. Anxiety isolates, trust erodes, and suspicion fractures community. In such moments, people become willing to surrender freedoms, conscience, and truth in exchange for the promise of safety. Crisis accelerates compliance. Fear becomes a tool of control when discernment is absent.

Global vulnerability is not new—but it is now visible. Systems built on efficiency rather than resilience falter under pressure. Supply chains snap under the weight of demand. Institutions contradict themselves. Experts disagree. Certainty dissolves. Pestilence reveals how quickly order gives way to confusion when the margin for error disappears. The world discovers it has been living on borrowed stability.

Yet Jesus does not frame pestilence as the end. Like war and creation's groaning, it is a birth pain. It's painful, disruptive, and unavoidable, but not meaningless. Birth pains force attention to an immediate need. They demand a response. They announce that the old way cannot continue unchanged. Something must be brought forth.

For the Church, pestilence is a proving ground. Will believers be ruled by fear or anchored in truth? Will love grow cold under pressure, or will compassion deepen? Scripture commands care for the sick, courage in uncertainty, and hope that does not

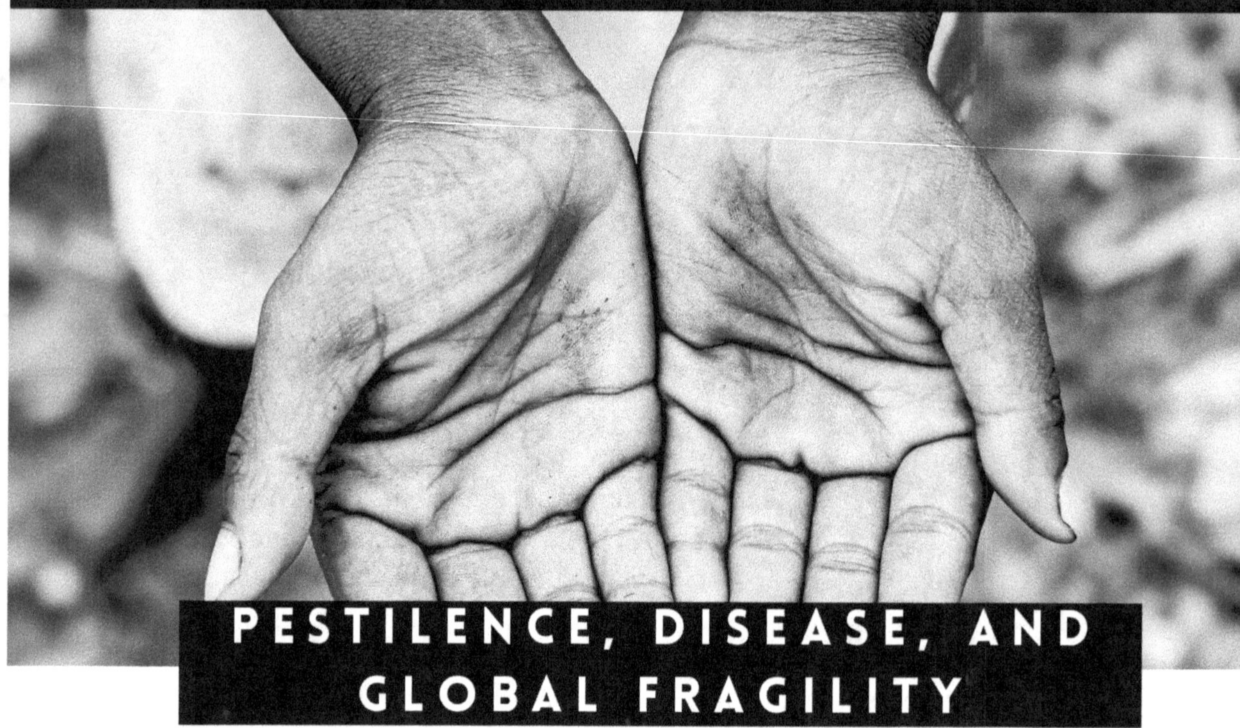

PESTILENCE, DISEASE, AND GLOBAL FRAGILITY

depend on circumstances. The people of God are not called to deny danger—but neither are they permitted to surrender to dread.

Disease tests our theology. It strips away shallow assurances and exposes whether faith rests in outcomes or in Christ Himself. It confronts believers with mortality and presses the eternal into present consciousness. In times of pestilence, the question is not whether life is fragile—we already know it is. The question is whether our hope is what is most fragile.

Jesus warned of pestilence not to frighten His followers, but to prepare them. Global instability is not proof that God has lost control. It is evidence that the world needs a Savior and is groaning for redemption. When systems fail and bodies weaken, the invitation remains the same: to repent, to endure, to love, and to lift our eyes beyond what is shaking.

These signs do not tell us to withdraw from the world, but to minister within it. They call the Church to be present, steady, truthful, and compassionate when everything else trembles. Pestilence reminds us that salvation was never meant to be found in health, longevity, or human order—but in Christ alone.

And as the world confronts its fragility, the people of God are called to demonstrate a different foundation—one that cannot be quarantined, shaken, or extinguished.

KEY SCRIPTURES

Please read the scriptures, then answer the questions that follow.

ONE

LUKE 21:11 NIV

"There will be great earthquakes, famines and pestilences in various places, and fearful events and great signs from heaven."

TWO

MATTHEW 24:8 NIV

"All these are the beginning of birth pains."

THREE

PSALM 91:1–6 NIV

"Whoever dwells in the shelter of the Most High will rest in the shadow of the Almighty. I will say of the Lord, 'He is my refuge and my fortress, my God, in whom I trust.' Surely he will save you from the fowler's snare and from the deadly pestilence. He will cover you with his feathers, and under his wings you will find refuge; his faithfulness will be your shield and rampart. You will not fear the terror of night, nor the arrow that flies by day, nor the pestilence that stalks in the darkness, nor the plague that destroys at midday."

FOUR

HEBREWS 12:26-27 NIV

"At that time his voice shook the earth, but now he has promised, 'Once more I will shake not only the earth but also the heavens.' The words 'once more' indicate the removing of what can be shaken—that is, created things—so that what cannot be shaken may remain."

FIVE

2 CORINTHIANS 4:16–18 NIV

"Therefore we do not lose heart. Though outwardly we are wasting away, yet inwardly we are being renewed day by day. For our light and momentary troubles are achieving for us an eternal glory that far outweighs them all. So we fix our eyes not on what is seen, but on what is unseen, since what is seen is temporary, but what is unseen is eternal."

NEXT

GROUP DISCUSSION QUESTIONS

CONSIDER THE SCRIPTURES READ, THEN ANSWER THE FOLLOWING QUESTIONS.

ASK YOURSELF...

Why did Jesus include pestilence as a sign of the last days? What does it reveal about human assumptions of control and stability?

How does fear function during times of disease, and how can it distort discernment?

What inequalities and moral fault lines does pestilence expose in societies today?

How should the Church respond during widespread illness and uncertainty?

How has recent global disease or crisis revealed where your confidence and trust were anchored?

WRITE YOUR ANSWERS HERE....

NEXT

GROUP DISCUSSION QUESTIONS

CONSIDER THE SCRIPTURES READ, THEN ANSWER THE FOLLOWING QUESTIONS.

ASK YOURSELF...

WRITE YOUR ANSWERS HERE....

In what ways does fear spread faster than truth during times of pestilence, and how can believers resist participating in fear-based narratives?

How does viewing disease and disruption as birth pains change the way we interpret suffering and uncertainty?

What practical responsibilities does the Church have during seasons of illness and instability that go beyond commentary or debate?

NEXT

Prayer

Father God,
Expose false confidence
and anchor us in Jesus alone.
We confess that too often we have trusted stability
more than You. Ground us in what cannot be shaken.
Give us discernment, compassion, and courage.
Teach us how to stand firm when systems
fail and to love well when fear dominates.
Guard our hearts from fear.
Teach us to love when safety is uncertain,
to speak truth when panic dominates,
and to hope when bodies weaken.
As the world confronts its fragility,
make us a people who stand firm—
present, compassionate, and unshaken—
bearing witness to Jesus Christ alone.
In the precious name of Jesus we pray,
Amen.

NEXT

CHAPTER 6 PERSECUTION LIKE NEVER BEFORE

"Then you will be handed over to be persecuted and put to death, and you will be hated by all nations because of Me."

—Matthew 24:9 NIV

PERSECUTION LIKE NEVER BEFORE

Jesus does not soften this warning. He does not qualify, spiritualize, or postpone it to another generation. He speaks plainly and directly: *"You will be…"* Persecution is not presented as a possibility but is announced as an expectation. Yet much of the modern Church treats persecution as an anomaly—something that happens somewhere else, in another time, or only to extremists. Jesus says otherwise. He places persecution at the center of His end-time teaching, not as an exception, but as part of the cost of following Him.

Scripture records persecution throughout history, so why does Jesus describe this coming wave as something unlike anything before it? Because this persecution will not be confined to a region or regime. It will be global and cultural, not local or merely governmental. It will involve social, economic, and ideological events, not only physical. It will be fueled not simply by the pursuit of power, but by moral accusation. *"You will be hated by all nations because of Me."* It will not be because of ignorance or misunderstanding but because of Christ Himself.

53

PERSECUTION LIKE NEVER BEFORE

This hatred will not always announce itself through immediate violence. Often it begins quietly—with exclusion, mockery, economic pressure, loss of platform, social isolation, and accusations of harm. Jesus prepared His disciples for this reality when He said, *"If the world hates you, keep in mind that it hated Me first."* [John 15:18, NIV] The hatred is not rational; it is spiritual. Truth confronts power. The light exposes darkness and darkness resists exposure.

As lawlessness increases, neutrality disappears. In stable societies, faith can coexist quietly. In collapsing societies, faith becomes a threat. Allegiance matters most when systems are fragile. Persecution escalates when moral lines sharpen, when truth becomes costly, and when obedience disrupts consensus. Scripture does not reserve this warning for radicals or extremists. Paul speaks plainly: *"Everyone who wants to live a godly life in Christ Jesus will be persecuted."* [2 Tim. 3:12, NIV] This is not a threat—it is a promise to the faithful.

Jesus immediately connects persecution with a sobering consequence: *"At that time many will turn away from the faith and will betray and hate each other."* [Matt. 24:10, NIV] Persecution does more than test endurance; it exposes the depth of belief. Some fall away not because faith was false, but because the cost became too high. The pressure clarifies priorities. What was once claimed publicly is reconsidered privately when consequences arrive.

One of the most painful features of end-time persecution is betrayal from within. Jesus warned of families divided, believers turning against believers, and communities fracturing under pressure. Jesus said plainly, *"Do not think that I have come to bring peace to the earth. I have not come to bring peace, but a sword. For I have come to set a man against his father, and a daughter against her mother, and a daughter-in-law against her mother-in-law. And a person's enemies will be those of his own household."* [Matt. 10:34-36, ESV] This betrayal is not driven by hatred alone, but by fear. Fear asks a devastating question: what will it cost me to stand with you?

The book of Revelation pulls back the curtain to reveal heaven's perspective. John writes, *"I saw under the altar the souls of those who had been slain because of the word of God and the testimony they had maintained."* [Rev. 6:9, NIV] Their suffering was not overlooked, and their witness was not forgotten. Persecution does not silence the Church—it purifies it. The blood of the martyrs has always been seed.

The question of why God allows persecution is difficult, but Scripture does not avoid it. Persecution refines our faith. It separates sincerity from convenience, strips away cultural Christianity, and forces allegiance into clarity. Jesus never promised safety; He promised His presence. *"I am with you always, even to the end of the age."* [Matthew 28:20, NIV] The promise is not an escape, but companionship through the fire.

Jesus offers one of the most sobering end-time declarations when He says, *"The one who stands firm to the end will be saved."* [Matthew 24:13, NIV] Endurance is not just passive survival. It is active faithfulness under pressure. The goal is not to avoid persecution, but to remain obedient through it.

Persecution does not ask what you believe. It asks what you are willing to lose. Belief that costs nothing has never been tested and faith that is never tested rarely endures.

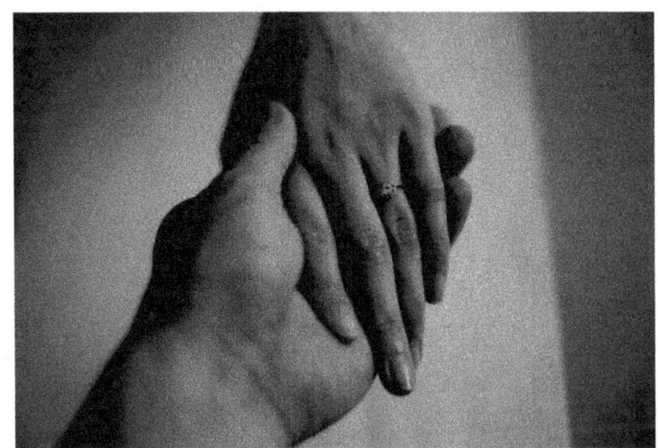

"AND SURELY I AM WITH YOU ALWAYS, TO THE VERY END OF THE AGE."
~MATT. 28:20 NIV

KEY SCRIPTURES

Please read the scriptures, then answer the questions that follow.

ONE

MATTHEW 24:9 NIV

"Then you will be handed over to be persecuted and put to death, and you will be hated by all nations because of me."

TWO

MATTHEW 24:10-13 NIV

"At that time many will turn away from the faith and will betray and hate each other, and many false prophets will appear and deceive many people. Because of the increase of wickedness, the love of most will grow cold, but the one who stands firm to the end will be saved."

THREE

JOHN 15:18-20 NIV

"If the world hates you, keep in mind that it hated me first. If you belonged to the world, it would love you as its own. As it is, you do not belong to the world, but I have chosen you out of the world. That is why the world hates you. Remember what I told you: 'A servant is not greater than his master.' If they persecuted me, they will persecute you also. If they obeyed my teaching, they will obey yours also."

FOUR

2 TIMOTHY 3:12 NIV

"In fact, everyone who wants to live a godly life in Christ Jesus will be persecuted."

FIVE

MATTHEW 10:34-36 NIV

"Do not suppose that I have come to bring peace to the earth. I did not come to bring peace, but a sword. For I have come to turn a man against his father, a daughter against her mother, a daughter-in-law against her mother-in-law—a man's enemies will be the members of his own household."

NEXT

PERSECUTION LIKE NEVER BEFORE

KEY SCRIPTURES

Please read the scriptures, then answer the questions that follow.

REVELATION 6:9–11 NIV

"When he opened the fifth seal, I saw under the altar the souls of those who had been slain because of the word of God and the testimony they had maintained. They called out in a loud voice, 'How long, Sovereign Lord, holy and true, until you judge the inhabitants of the earth and avenge our blood?' Then each of them was given a white robe, and they were told to wait a little longer, until the full number of their fellow servants, their brothers and sisters, were killed just as they had been."

ACTS 14:22 NIV

"Strengthening the disciples and encouraging them to remain true to the faith. 'We must go through many hardships to enter the kingdom of God,' they said."

1 PETER 4:12–16 NIV

"Dear friends, do not be surprised at the fiery ordeal that has come on you to test you, as though something strange were happening to you. But rejoice inasmuch as you participate in the sufferings of Christ, so that you may be overjoyed when his glory is revealed. If you are insulted because of the name of Christ, you are blessed, for the Spirit of glory and of God rests on you. If you suffer, it should not be as a murderer or thief or any other kind of criminal, or even as a meddler. However, if you suffer as a Christian, do not be ashamed, but praise God that you bear that name."

HEBREWS 10:34–38 NIV

"You suffered along with those in prison and joyfully accepted the confiscation of your property, because you knew that you yourselves had better and lasting possessions. So do not throw away your confidence; it will be richly rewarded. You need to persevere so that when you have done the will of God, you will receive what he has promised. For 'In just a little while, he who is coming will come and will not delay.' And, 'But my righteous one will live by faith. and I take no pleasure in the one who shrinks back.'"

MATTHEW 28:20 NIV

"And teaching them to obey everything I have commanded you. And surely I am with you always, to the very end of the age."

NEXT

GROUP DISCUSSION QUESTIONS

CONSIDER THE SCRIPTURES READ, THEN ANSWER THE FOLLOWING QUESTIONS.

Why does Jesus place persecution at the center of His end-times teaching?

What does this reveal about the nature of discipleship?

How does modern culture subtly discourage faithfulness without overt violence?

Where do you see "quiet persecution" at work?

Why does persecution often lead to betrayal within families and communities?

NEXT

GROUP DISCUSSION QUESTIONS

CONSIDER THE SCRIPTURES READ, THEN ANSWER THE FOLLOWING QUESTIONS.

With family or community betrayal, How does fear influence loyalty?

1

What does it mean to "stand firm to the end" in practical, everyday terms?

2

What forms of pressure against faith exist today?

3

How can we build spiritual resilience before persecution intensifies?

4

NEXT

Prayer

Dear Heavenly Father,
Forgive us for expecting comfort where You
promised a cross. Strengthen our hearts for
endurance, our love for truth, and our courage to
remain faithful when obedience is expensive.
Prepare us for pressure without panic, for
opposition without hatred, and for loss without
despair. When fear whispers compromise, anchor us
in Your presence.
When loyalty is tested, keep us standing firm.
We choose faithfulness over safety and allegiance
over approval.
Be with us to the end of the age,
as You promised. We pray this in the name of
Jesus.
Amen.

CHAPTER 7
THE GREAT FALLING AWAY

NEXT

"Let no one deceive you in any way. For that day will not come, unless the rebellion comes first, and the man of lawlessness is revealed, the son of destruction."

—*2 Thessalonians 2:3 NIV*

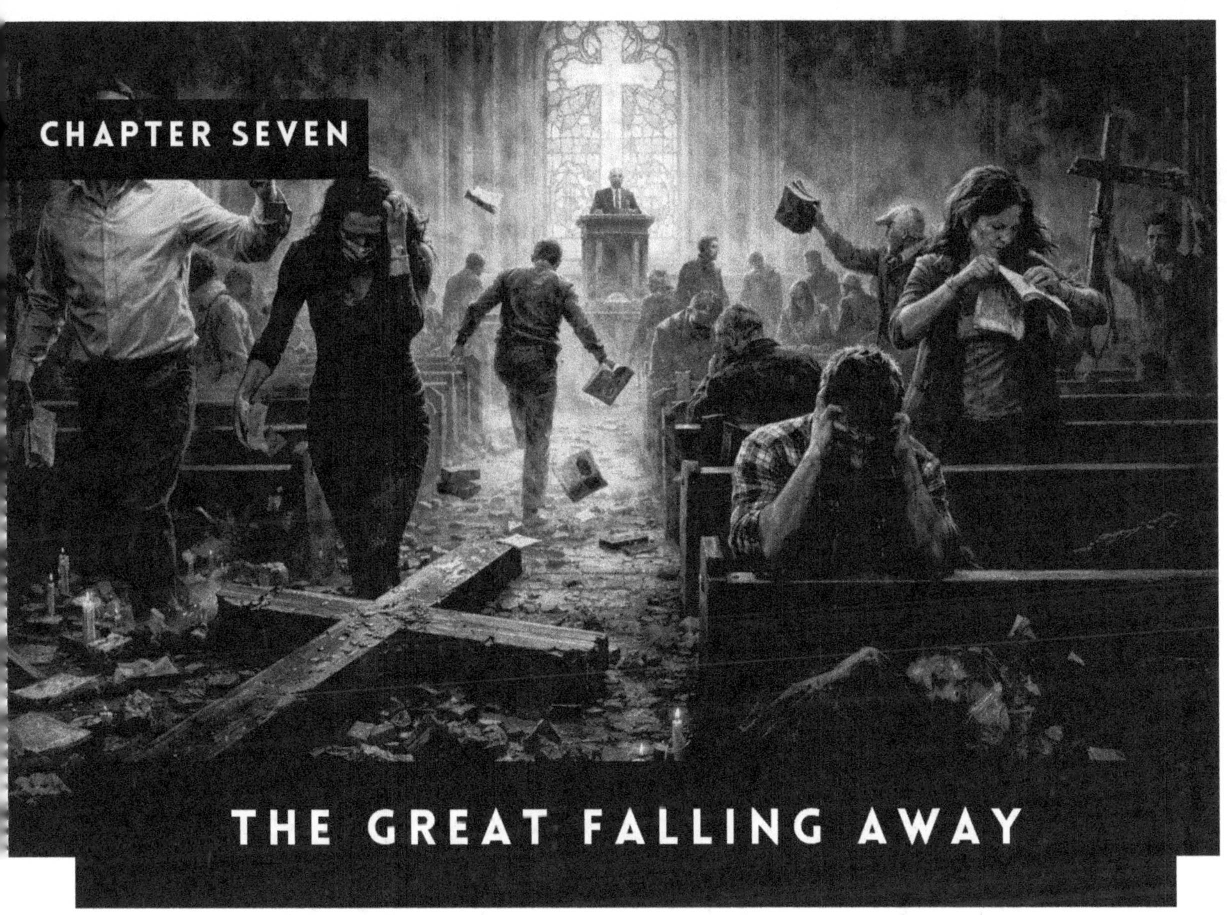

THE GREAT FALLING AWAY

Scripture does not describe the last days as a season of uninterrupted revival alone. It also describes a great separation. The apostle Paul names it without hesitation: the falling away—a rebellion and an apostasy. This is a phrase we often prefer not to hear because it confronts us with an uncomfortable truth. The end will not only reveal faith; it will also expose defection. This falling away is not a momentary lapse of interest, a season of doubt, or pressure applied from the outside alone. It is a deliberate departure from truth by those who once stood close enough to recognize it.

The Great Falling Away does not primarily concern those who never believed. It speaks to those who knew the language of faith, participated in religious life, benefited from Christian community, and possessed enough understanding to identify the truth when it was presented. Jesus said plainly, *"At that time many will turn away from the faith."* [Matt. 24:10, NIV] Turning away implies proximity. One cannot abandon what was never known.

63

THE GREAT FALLING AWAY

This apostasy forms at the intersection of persecution and deception. Persecution applies pressure. Deception offers relief. When obedience becomes costly, deception presents alternatives—a softer gospel, a privatized faith, a redefined truth, or a version of Christianity that avoids offense and demands nothing. Paul warned Timothy that people would *"gather teachers to say what their itching ears want to hear."* [2 Timothy 4:3, NIV] Deception thrives wherever trust and endurance is absent.

Pressure does not create unbelief; it reveals what belief was rooted in all along. Faith built on comfort, social approval, moral superiority, or cultural alignment collapses when it begins to cost something. Jesus described this dynamic long before the end times when He said, *"When trouble or persecution comes because of the word, they quickly fall away."* [Matt. 13:21 NIV] The cost exposes their foundations.

Apostasy rarely announces itself as rebellion. It often sounds reasonable, compassionate, even virtuous. It speaks in the language of love without truth, compassion without repentance, unity without holiness, and peace without Christ. Paul explains that the deception is not subtle because truth was unavailable, but because truth was unwanted. *"They perish because they refused to love the truth and so be saved."* [2 Thess. 2:10 NIV] The issue is not information but affection.

Jesus connects the falling away with betrayal. *"Many will turn away...and will betray and hate each other."* [Matthew 24:10 NIV] Betrayal emerges when standing with the faithful becomes dangerous. Fear reframes loyalty as a liability. What once would have been unthinkable becomes justifiable in the name of survival. Conviction is slowly traded for self-preservation.

Paul describes this rebellion as something that must occur before Christ's return. It is not isolated or accidental. It is global and systemic. Across cultures, truth becomes inconvenient. Holiness becomes offensive. Biblical authority turns intolerable. The world does not merely reject Christ—it pressures believers to do the rejecting for themselves.

NEXT

THE GREAT FALLING AWAY

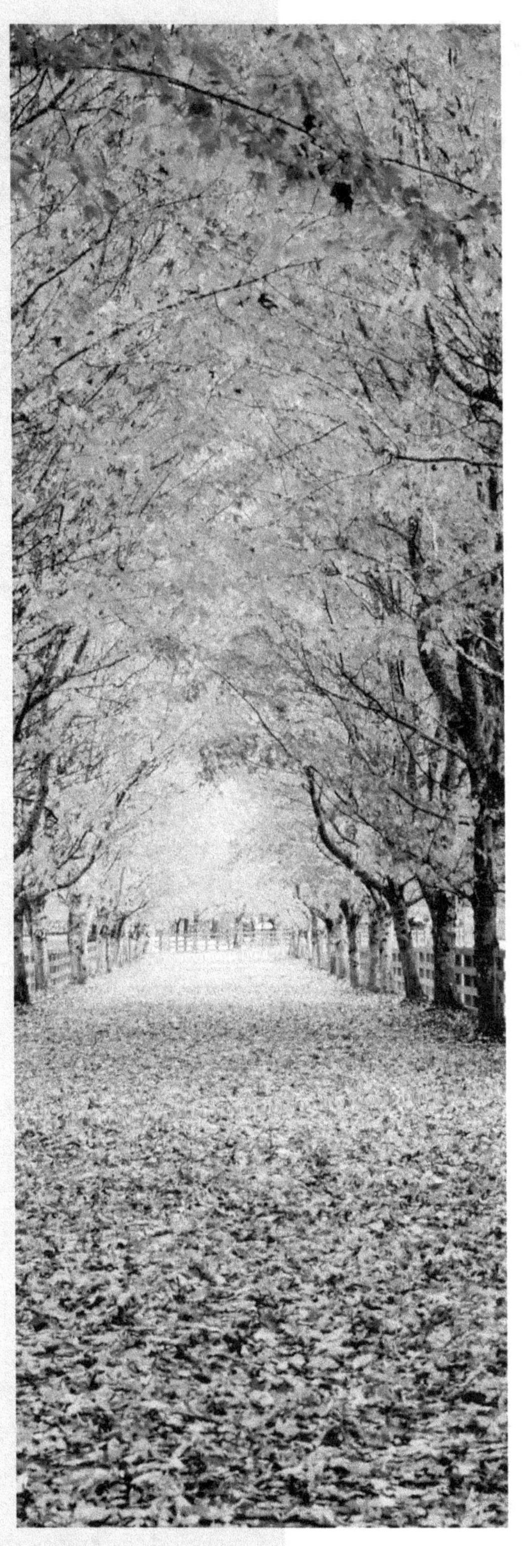

In contrast, Jesus defines saving faith not by avoidance, but by endurance. He does not say, "The one who escapes conflict will be saved." He says, *"The one who stands firm to the end will be saved."* *[Matt. 24:13 NIV]* Enduring faith is marked by conviction without cruelty, love without compromise, courage without arrogance, and obedience without applause. Endurance becomes the dividing line.

The Great Falling Away ultimately presses one unavoidable question upon every heart: is Christ worth obedience when it costs everything else? Those who answer yes will stand. Those who answer no will drift —often sincerely, often sorrowfully, but decisively. This is not a question of perfection, but of allegiance.

The Hebrews writer issues both a warning and a promise. *"See to it... that none of you has a sinful, unbelieving heart that turns away from the living God."* *[Hebrews 3:12]* Yet it also declares hope: *"We have come to share in Christ, if indeed we hold our original conviction firmly to the very end."* *[Hebrews 3:14]* The falling away is real but so is endurance and by the grace of God, endurance is possible.

65

THE GREAT FALLING AWAY

Please read the scriptures, then answer the questions that follow.

ONE

2 THESSALONIANS 2:3 NIV

"Don't let anyone deceive you in any way, for that day will not come until the rebellion occurs and the man of lawlessness is revealed, the man doomed to destruction."

TWO

MATTHEW 24:10, 13 NIV

"At that time many will turn away from the faith and will betray and hate each other, but the one who stands firm to the end will be saved."

THREE

MATTHEW 13:20–21 NIV

"The seed falling on rocky ground refers to someone who hears the word and at once receives it with joy. But since they have no root, they last only a short time. When trouble or persecution comes because of the word, they quickly fall away."

FOUR

2 TIMOTHY 4:3–4 NIV

"For the time will come when people will not put up with sound doctrine. Instead, to suit their own desires, they will gather around them a great number of teachers to say what their itching ears want to hear. They will turn their ears away from the truth and turn aside to myths."

FIVE

2 THESSALONIANS 2:9–12 NIV

"The coming of the lawless one will be in accordance with how Satan works. He will use all sorts of displays of power through signs and wonders that serve the lie, and all the ways that wickedness deceives those who are perishing. They perish because they refused to love the truth and so be saved. For this reason God sends them a powerful delusion so that they will believe the lie and so that all will be condemned who have not believed the truth but have delighted in wickedness."

NEXT

THE GREAT FALLING AWAY

Please read the scriptures, then answer the questions that follow.

ONE

HEBREWS 3:12–14 NIV

"See to it, brothers and sisters, that none of you has a sinful, unbelieving heart that turns away from the living God. But encourage one another daily, as long as it is called 'Today,' so that none of you may be hardened by sin's deceitfulness. We have come to share in Christ, if indeed we hold our original conviction firmly to the very end."

TWO

HEBREWS 10:37–39 NIV

"For, 'In just a little while, he who is coming will come and will not delay.' And, 'But my righteous one will live by faith. And I take no pleasure in the one who shrinks back.' But we do not belong to those who shrink back and are destroyed, but to those who have faith and are saved."

THREE

JOHN 6:66–69 NIV

"From this time many of his disciples turned back and no longer followed him. 'You do not want to leave too, do you?' Jesus asked the Twelve. Simon Peter answered him, 'Lord, to whom shall we go? You have the words of eternal life. We have come to believe and to know that you are the Holy One of God.'"

FOUR

1 JOHN 2:19 NIV

"They went out from us, but they did not really belong to us. For if they had belonged to us, they would have remained with us; but their going showed that none of them belonged to us."

FIVE

JUDE 3–4 NIV

"Dear friends, although I was very eager to write to you about the salvation we share, I felt compelled to write and urge you to contend for the faith that was once for all entrusted to God's holy people. For certain individuals whose condemnation was written about long ago have secretly slipped in among you. They are ungodly people, who pervert the grace of our God into a license for immorality and deny Jesus Christ our only Sovereign and Lord."

67

NEXT

GROUP DISCUSSION QUESTIONS

CONSIDER THE SCRIPTURES READ, THEN ANSWER THE FOLLOWING QUESTIONS.

ASK YOURSELF...

WRITE YOUR ANSWERS HERE....

Why does Scripture insist that a great falling away must occur before Christ's return?

What does this reveal about the nature of faith under pressure?

How does persecution and deception work together to produce apostasy?

Why does apostasy often present itself as compassion or progress rather than rebellion?

What practical habits help believers remain anchored when truth becomes costly?

NEXT

GROUP DISCUSSION QUESTIONS

CONSIDER THE SCRIPTURES READ, THEN ANSWER THE FOLLOWING QUESTIONS.

ASK YOURSELF...

WRITE YOUR ANSWERS HERE....

Why is the idea of a "great falling away" difficult for the modern Church to confront honestly?

What are examples of "reasonable-sounding" departures from truth that believers may face today?

What does endurance look like when obedience costs relationships, reputation, or security?

69

NEXT

Prayer

Faithful God,

Search our hearts. Expose every place where comfort competes with obedience and approval rivals allegiance. Strengthen our resolve. Anchor us in truth so that we are heart possessors and not mouth confessors only.

Give us endurance that does not waver and love that does not compromise.

Strengthen us to endure without bitterness, to love without compromise, and to obey without applause. When pressure rises and deception whispers relief, ground us in Christ alone. By Your grace, help us hold fast to our original conviction to the very end.

Above all, we choose You—
not only in word, but in our obedience,
to the very end.

In Jesus's name we pray,

Amen.

CHAPTER 8
FALSE PROPHETS, LAWLESSNESS, AND LOVE GROWS COLD

"And many false prophets will arise and lead many astray. And because lawlessness will be increased, the love of many will grow cold."

—Matthew 24:11-12 ESV

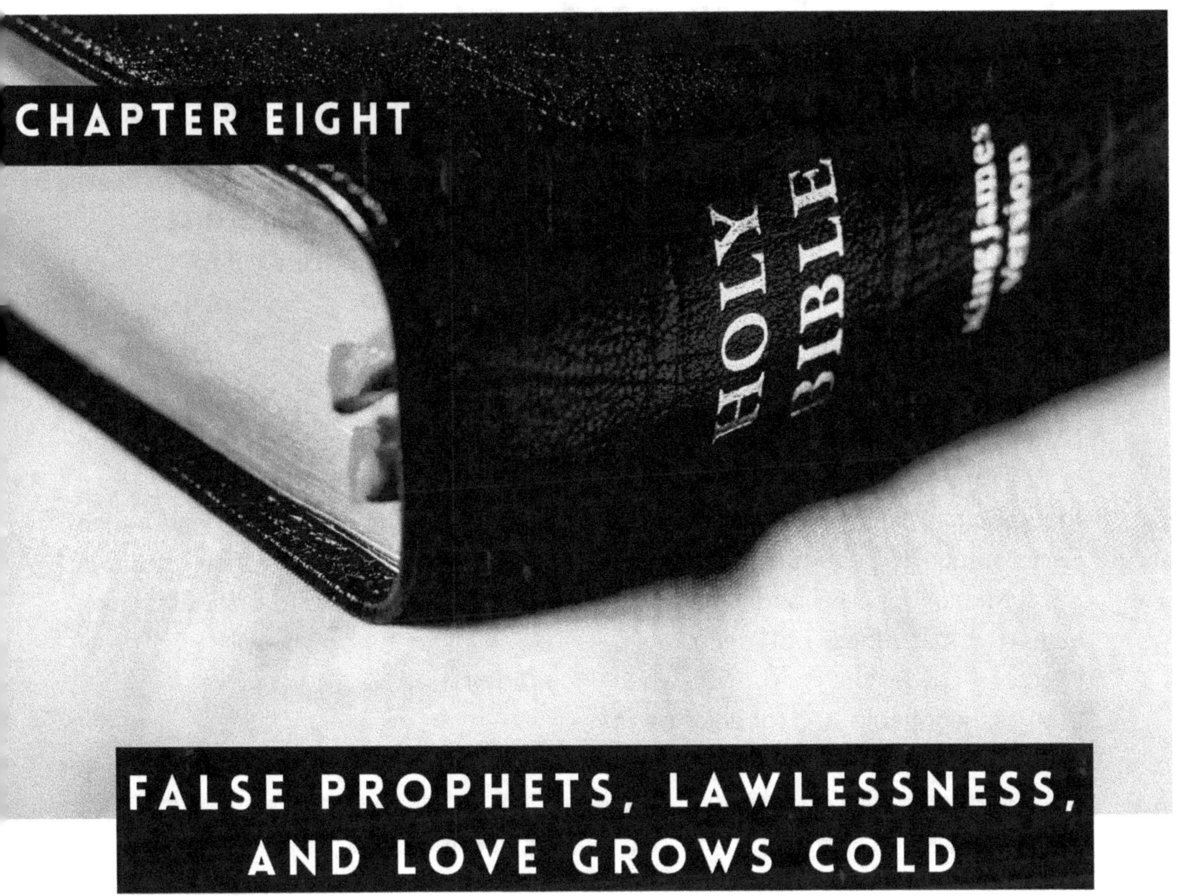

FALSE PROPHETS, LAWLESSNESS, AND LOVE GROWS COLD

Jesus warns that as pressure increases, deception will multiply. The proliferation of false prophets intensify in times of crisis. Confusion creates demand for certainty, and wherever people are desperate for answers, counterfeit voices rush in to fill the vacuum. False prophets do not always deny God outright. More often, they distort His character, dilute His commands, or redefine righteousness to fit the spirit of the age. They speak in spiritual language while severing truth from obedience, offering reassurance without repentance and hope without holiness.

False prophets thrive where discernment weakens. They flourish in environments shaped by emotionalism, community or political loyalty, and selective listening. Scripture warns that many will be led astray—not because truth was unavailable, but because truth became inconvenient. False prophecy often tells people what they want to hear rather than what they need to hear. It trades the narrow way for broad approval and substitutes affirmation for transformation.

NEXT

FALSE PROPHETS, LAWLESSNESS, AND LOVE GROWS COLD

"For false prophets will arise and lead many astray. And because lawlessness will increase, the love of many will grow cold."
—Matthew 24:11–12 ESV

As false prophecy spreads, lawlessness increases. Lawlessness is not merely criminal behavior; it is the rejection of God's moral order. It is resistance to restraint, disdain for accountability, and hostility toward authority that does not serve self-interest. Lawlessness grows when truth is negotiable and obedience is optional. When God's standards are dismissed as outdated or oppressive, chaos follows. It's when boundaries erode, conscience dulls, and right and wrong blur into preference.

Jesus connects lawlessness directly to a chilling consequence: the love of many grows cold. Love does not disappear all at once; it cools gradually. Compassion is replaced with calculation. Mercy yields to fatigue. Loyalty weakens under pressure. When survival becomes the priority, love becomes expendable. Cold love still speaks kindly, but it no longer sacrifices. It still claims faith, but it avoids any cost.

This cooling of love is one of the most dangerous signs of the end because it happens quietly—even among believers. Love grows cold when righteousness is reduced to ideology, when truth is wielded without humility, and when endurance is mistaken for indifference. Jesus is not describing a world that hates love; He is describing a people who grow tired of it.

False prophets exploit this fatigue. They offer spiritual shortcuts that require less sacrifice, less endurance, and less holiness. They promise relief from the tension of obedience and provide permission to disengage emotionally. In doing so, they normalize distance, numbness, and disengagement as wisdom.

Yet Jesus does not leave His followers without instruction. He contrasts growing cold with steadfast endurance. Love that endures is not sentimental but disciplined. It is rooted in obedience, sustained by truth, and empowered by the Holy Spirit. Enduring love does not burn hot with emotion one day and disappear the next. It remains faithful when affection fades and when sacrifice is costly.

NEXT

FALSE PROPHETS, LAWLESSNESS, AND LOVE GROWS COLD

The tragedy of the last days is not merely deception or lawlessness—it is lovelessness. A church that retains correct doctrine but loses active love ceases to reflect Christ. Paul warned the church in Ephesus of this very danger: truth without love is still a departure. Adherence to the letter of the law without affection is not faithfulness.

The call of the hour is not to out-argue false prophets or outshout lawlessness, but to remain anchored in truth and love. Love that refuses compromise. Love that endures misunderstanding. Love that does not grow cold when hatred increases. This is the love that will mark those who belong to Christ at the end.

Jesus does not ask whether deception will increase, whether lawlessness will spread, or whether love will be tested. He tells us it will. The question that remains is not what the world will do but whether our love will endure to the end.

"By this everyone will know that you are my disciples, if you love one another."
~ John 13:35 NIV

FALSE PROPHETS, LAWLESSNESS, AND LOVE GROWS COLD

KEY SCRIPTURES

Please read the scriptures, then answer the questions that follow.

ONE

MATTHEW 24:11–12 ESV

"And many false prophets will appear and deceive many people. Because of the increase of wickedness, the love of most will grow cold."

TWO

MATTHEW 24:13 NIV

"But the one who stands firm to the end will be saved."

THREE

2 TIMOTHY 4:3–4 NIV

"For the time will come when people will not put up with sound doctrine. Instead, to suit their own desires, they will gather around them a great number of teachers to say what their itching ears want to hear. They will turn their ears away from the truth and turn aside to myths."

FOUR

JEREMIAH 23:16–17 NIV

"This is what the Lord Almighty says: 'Do not listen to what the prophets are prophesying to you; they fill you with false hopes. They speak visions from their own minds, not from the mouth of the Lord. They keep saying to those who despise me, 'The Lord says: You will have peace.' And to all who follow the stubbornness of their hearts they say, 'No harm will come to you.'"

FIVE

1 JOHN 4:1 NIV

"Dear friends, do not believe every spirit, but test the spirits to see whether they are from God, because many false prophets have gone out into the world."

FALSE PROPHETS, LAWLESSNESS, AND LOVE GROWS COLD

KEY SCRIPTURES

Please read the scriptures, then answer the questions that follow.

ONE

ISAIAH 5:20 NIV

"Woe to those who call evil good and good evil, who put darkness for light and light for darkness, who put bitter for sweet and sweet for bitter."

TWO

ROMANS 1:28–32 NIV

"They have become filled with every kind of wickedness, evil, greed and depravity. They are full of envy, murder, strife, deceit and malice. They are gossips, slanderers, God-haters, insolent, arrogant and boastful; they invent ways of doing evil; they disobey their parents; they have no understanding, no fidelity, no love, no mercy. Although they know God's righteous decree that those who do such things deserve death, they not only continue to do these very things but also approve of those who practice them."

THREE

1 CORINTHIANS 13:1–3 NIV

"If I speak in the tongues of men or of angels, but do not have love, I am only a resounding gong or a clanging cymbal. If I have the gift of prophecy and can fathom all mysteries and all knowledge, and if I have a faith that can move mountains, but do not have love, I am nothing. If I give all I possess to the poor and give over my body to hardship that I may boast, but do not have love, I gain nothing."

GALATIANS 5:22–23 NIV

"But the fruit of the Spirit is love, joy, peace, forbearance, kindness, goodness, faithfulness, gentleness and self-control. Against such things there is no law."

FOUR

FIVE

HEBREWS 10:24–25 NIV

"And let us consider how we may spur one another on toward love and good deeds, not giving up meeting together, as some are in the habit of doing, but encouraging one another—and all the more as you see the Day approaching."

NEXT

GROUP DISCUSSION QUESTIONS

CONSIDER THE SCRIPTURES READ, THEN ANSWER THE FOLLOWING QUESTIONS.

ONE
How can false prophets sound comforting while quietly leading people away from obedience?

TWO
What makes false prophets message appealing? What are modern examples?

THREE
How does lawlessness differ from open rebellion—and why is it harder to recognize?

FOUR
What does it look like for love to "grow cold" without disappearing entirely—especially within the Church?

FIVE
What are the warning signs that love is "cooling" rather than enduring?

SIX
How can believers hold truth firmly without allowing love to harden or withdraw under pressure?

SEVEN
In what ways does lawlessness show up culturally or spiritually beyond obvious criminal behavior?

NEXT

Dear Father,

We confess that fatigue, fear,
and pressure have sometimes cooled our hearts.
Restore our love.
Sharpen our discernment.
Anchor us in your love that does not retreat.
Search our hearts.
Expose every place where fatigue cools compassion
and convenience dulls obedience.
Guard us from shortcuts that promise relief
but steal holiness.
Protect us from voices that soothe without sanctifying
and comfort us without calling us higher.
Give us endurance that remains obedient
and love that remains active—until the end.
When pressure rises and voices multiply,
keep us discerning.
When hatred grows louder,
keep our love warm—
faithful, sacrificial, and rooted in You.
May our love endure to the end,
so the world may see Christ in us.
In Jesus's name we pray,
Amen.

NEXT

CHAPTER 9
THE GOSPEL REACHES THE ENTIRE WORLD

"And this gospel of
the kingdom will be
preached in the
whole world as a
testimony to all
nations, and then
the end will come."

—Matthew 24:14 NIV

THE GOSPEL REACHES THE ENTIRE WORLD

In the middle of dire warnings—persecution, deception, falling away, and love growing cold—Jesus does something startling. He interrupts the darkness with a declaration of unstoppable hope. Before the end comes, the Gospel will be preached to the whole world. It will not be the gospel of comfort, the gospel of nationalism, not even the gospel of self-fulfillment or self-help. But the Gospel of the Kingdom of God will be preached globally. This verse is a divine interruption. It announces that chaos does not get the final word—Christ does.

Jesus is careful about what He does not say. He does not say the world will improve first. He does not say persecution must stop or unity must be perfected. He does not say order must be restored before proclamation can proceed. He says the Gospel will advance in the middle of disorder. Darkness does not delay the mission. It accelerates it. Crisis does not silence the message. It amplifies it.

NEXT

THE GOSPEL REACHES THE ENTIRE WORLD

"And this gospel of the kingdom will be preached in the whole world as a testimony to all nations, and then the end will come."
—Matthew 24:14 NIV

This distinction matters, because Jesus does not speak merely of the gospel of personal salvation, though salvation is central. He declares the Gospel of the Kingdom. This Gospel announces that Jesus is King, that His reign is righteous, that His authority supersedes every nation, and that His justice outlasts every empire. It is not only about forgiveness of sins; it is about allegiance. It confronts every throne, every ideology, and every identity that demands ultimate loyalty.

Jesus is precise about the outcome. The Gospel will be preached as a testimony to all nations. He does not say all nations will repent. He says all nations will hear. Testimony means witness. When history closes, the world will not be able to claim ignorance. No one will be able to say, "We did not know," "We were not warned," or "We never heard." Before judgment comes, truth is announced. Before the end arrives, true witness is given.

This global testimony intensifies near the end because collapsing systems create open ears. Fear loosens certainty. Instability awakens questions. Suffering exposes false saviors. But the end of the age is not marked only by rebellion. It is also marked by harvest.

For the first time in human history, the Gospel is moving with unprecedented speed. Language barriers are falling. Scripture is accessible across the globe. Messages travel instantly and persecution cannot silence testimony. What governments restrict, God reroutes. What systems censor, the Spirit multiplies. The Gospel is no longer confined to pulpits. It moves through whispers and screens, through prisons and exile, and through suffering saints and unseen witnesses.

The Church, therefore, is not called to predict the end. It is called to proclaim Christ until the end comes. This proclamation must be bold without arrogance, compassionate without dilution, and faithful without fear. Paul asks the question that still governs the mission: *"How can they believe in the one of whom they have not heard?"* [Rom. 10:14 NIV] The assignment has not changed—only

THE GOSPEL REACHES THE ENTIRE WORLD

the urgency has increased.

Opposition intensifies precisely because the Gospel advances. It threatens power built on lies, economies built on exploitation, and identities built on false worship. Resistance is not evidence of failure; it is confirmation. The Gospel does not advance because the world welcomes it. It advances because God has decreed it.

Jesus ties the conclusion of history not to political victory, moral reform, or human achievement, but to witness. The proclamation of the Gospel precedes completion of this age. God ensures that every generation has the opportunity to respond. Judgment never arrives without testimony.

And this leaves us with a question that cannot be avoided. The Gospel reaching the world does not excuse passivity. It demands positioning. Where are you placed in this final witness? Are you a carrier of the message, a supporter of those who go, or a bystander watching history unfold? In case you didn't know, silence speaks, too.

"But you will receive power when the Holy Spirit comes on you; and you will be my witnesses in Jerusalem, and in all Judea and Samaria, and to the ends of the earth."
~ Acts 1:8 NIV

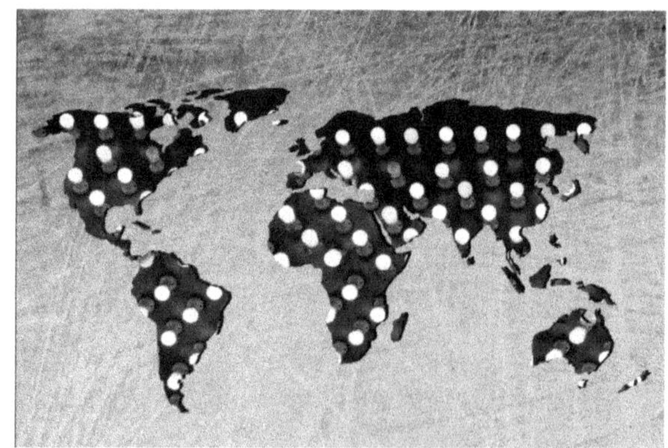

NEXT

KEY SCRIPTURES

Please read the scriptures, then answer the questions that follow.

ONE

MATTHEW 24:14 NIV

"And this gospel of the kingdom will be preached in the whole world as a testimony to all nations, and then the end will come."

TWO

MATTHEW 24:9–13 NIV

"Then you will be handed over to be persecuted and put to death, and you will be hated by all nations because of me. At that time many will turn away from the faith and will betray and hate each other, and many false prophets will appear and deceive many people. Because of the increase of wickedness, the love of most will grow cold, but the one who stands firm to the end will be saved."

THREE

MATTHEW 28:18–20 NIV

"Then Jesus came to them and said, 'All authority in heaven and on earth has been given to me. Therefore go and make disciples of all nations, baptizing them in the name of the Father and of the Son and of the Holy Spirit, and teaching them to obey everything I have commanded you. And surely I am with you always, to the very end of the age.'"

FOUR

ROMANS 10:14–15 NIV

"How, then, can they call on the one they have not believed in? And how can they believe in the one of whom they have not heard? And how can they hear without someone preaching to them? And how can anyone preach unless they are sent? As it is written: 'How beautiful are the feet of those who bring good news!'"

FIVE

REVELATION 7:9–10 NIV

"After this I looked, and there before me was a great multitude that no one could count, from every nation, tribe, people and language, standing before the throne and before the Lamb. They were wearing white robes and were holding palm branches in their hands. And they cried out in a loud voice: 'Salvation belongs to our God, who sits on the throne, and to the Lamb.'"

NEXT

KEY SCRIPTURES

Please read the scriptures, then answer the questions that follow.

ONE

COLOSSIANS 1:5–6 NIV

"The faith and love that spring from the hope stored up for you in heaven and about which you have already heard in the true message of the gospel that has come to you. In the same way, the gospel is bearing fruit and growing throughout the whole world—just as it has been doing among you since the day you heard it and truly understood God's grace."

TWO

ACTS 1:8 NIV

"But you will receive power when the Holy Spirit comes on you; and you will be my witnesses in Jerusalem, and in all Judea and Samaria, and to the ends of the earth."

THREE

ISAIAH 52:7 NIV

"How beautiful on the mountains are the feet of those who bring good news, who proclaim peace, who bring good tidings, who proclaim salvation, who say to Zion, 'Your God reigns!'"

FOUR

PSALM 96:3 NIV

"Declare his glory among the nations, his marvelous deeds among all peoples."

FIVE

HABAKKUK 2:14 NIV

"For the earth will be filled with the knowledge of the glory of the Lord as the waters cover the sea."

NEXT

GROUP DISCUSSION QUESTIONS

CONSIDER THE SCRIPTURES READ, THEN ANSWER THE FOLLOWING QUESTIONS.

ONE
Why does Jesus declare a global gospel proclamation immediately before the end? What does this reveal about God's character?

TWO
How does the Gospel of the Kingdom differ from any other gospel?

THREE
Why does resistance often increase when the Gospel advances? What does opposition confirm rather than negate?

FOUR
Where do you see yourself positioned in the global witness—carrier, supporter, or observer?

FIVE
How does understanding the gospel of the Kingdom change the way we view evangelism and discipleship?

SIX
What does it mean that the Gospel is preached as a testimony, not a guarantee of global repentance?

SEVEN
Where do you see darkness accelerating—not hindering—the spread of the Gospel today?

NEXT

Prayer

Father God,

We confess that fear, distraction,
and comfort have sometimes muted our witness.
Reignite our urgency. Clarify our assignment.
Anchor us in the Gospel of Your Kingdom. Align our
hearts with Your Truth. Strip away comfort-
centered faith and ground us in allegiance to You
alone. Give us courage to speak, humility to serve,
and endurance to remain faithful until our witness
is complete. Where You have planted us, make us
bold carriers of truth—not silent observers of history.
We pray that we will be found proclaiming Christ
when the end comes, not watching from a
distance.
For Yours is the Kingdom,
the power, and the glory,
forever.
Amen.

CHAPTER 10
THE ABOMINATION THAT CAUSES DESOLATION

NEXT

"So when you see standing in the holy place 'the abomination that causes desolation,' spoken of through the prophet Daniel—let the reader understand."

—MATTHEW 24:15 NIV

NEXT

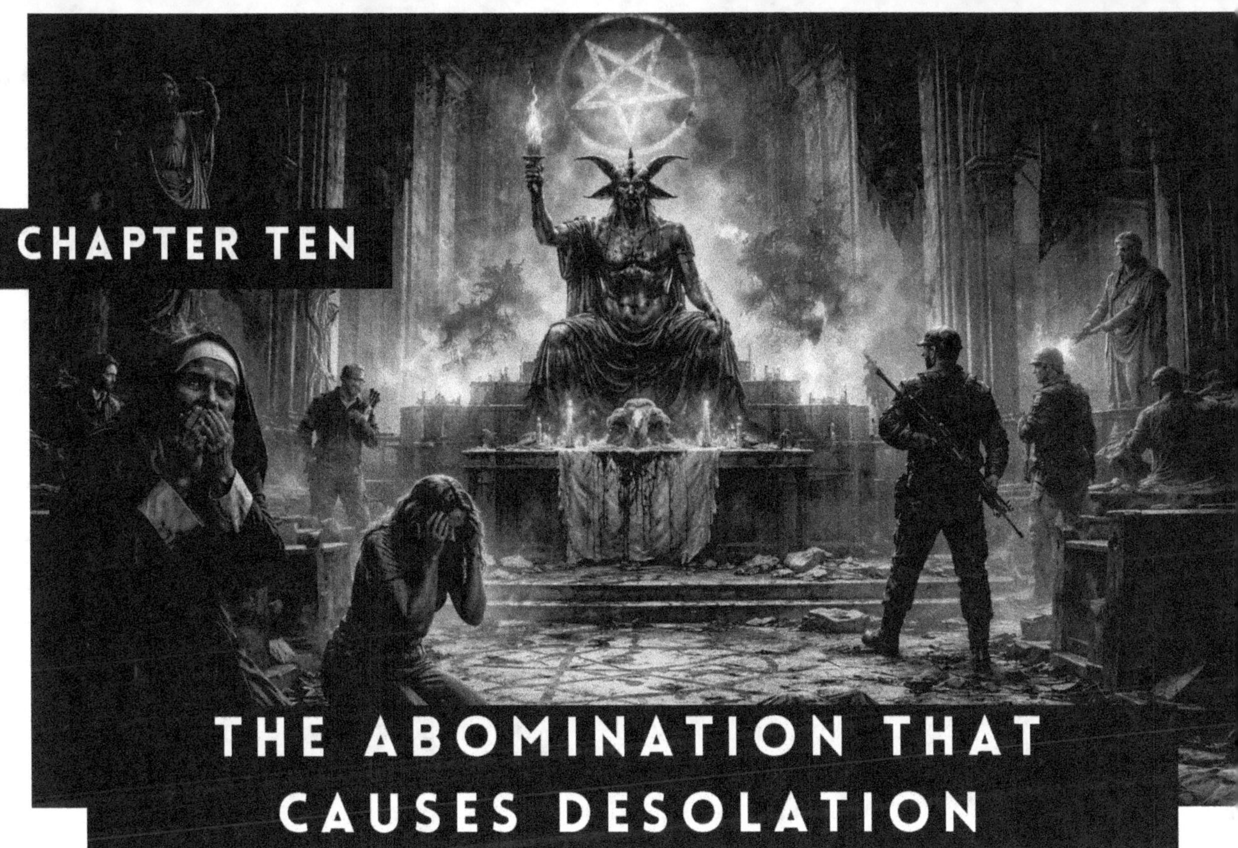

THE ABOMINATION THAT CAUSES DESOLATION

In the midst of His end-time teaching, Jesus pauses and delivers a command that is both rare and arresting: "Let the reader understand." Jesus is not "waxing poetic" or inserting symbolic filler. It is an urgent directive meant to be recognized in real time. Jesus is telling His followers that discernment will be required—because what He is describing will be unmistakable to those who know the Scriptures. The abomination that causes desolation is not a vague spiritual feeling or a private revelation. It is a decisive prophetic marker. When it appears, the season shifts.

Jesus does not say if you see it. He says when. And He deliberately anchors His warning in the writings of Daniel, invoking prophecy that had already proven true in history. Daniel foretold a moment when sacred worship would be violated, authority usurped, and covenant faith trampled. *"Forces from him shall appear and profane the temple and fortress and shall take away the regular burnt offering. And they shall set up the abomination that makes desolate."* [Daniel 11:31 ESV] This was not abstract theology. It was concrete history.

In 167 B.C., that prophecy found a terrifying fulfillment under Antiochus IV Epiphanes. (Encyclopedia.com, 2026) He halted the daily sacrifices in Jerusalem, defiled the holy place, and erected a pagan altar—traditionally understood to be dedicated to Zeus—within the Temple itself.

NEXT

THE ABOMINATION THAT CAUSES DESOLATION

"So when you see standing in the holy place 'the abomination that causes desolation,' spoken of through the prophet Daniel—let the reader understand."
—Matthew 24:15 NIV

The Temple was violated. True worship was outlawed. A counterfeit demanded allegiance. The Jewish people immediately recognized this act as the abomination Daniel had warned about. Desolation followed, not because God was absent, but because what was holy had been deliberately profaned.

Jesus draws directly from this historical memory to warn of a future escalation. He signals continuity and intensification. What happened under Antiochus was not the final fulfillment —it was a foreshadowing. It was a preview and a prophetic pattern. Just as Daniel's words came true in history, Jesus declares they will come true again—on a greater, more decisive scale.

In Scripture, an abomination is never merely something offensive. It is something detestable to God, corrupting to worship, and destructive to covenant faithfulness. Abominations always involve false worship. They demand allegiance where none is due. They replace devotion to God with submission to a counterfeit authority.

Desolation is the inevitable result. When the place where God dwells is violated, worship collapses, truth is displaced, and spiritual life drains from what once held meaning. Desolation leaves people barren— confused, displaced, and vulnerable. What was meant to be a place of encounter between heaven and earth becomes a site of abandonment.

"When you see 'the abomination that causes desolation' standing where it does not belong—let the reader understand— then let those who are in Judea flee to the mountains."
~ Mark 13:14 NIV

NEXT

THE ABOMINATION THAT CAUSES DESOLATION

Jesus locates this future event in "the holy place," and the apostle Paul echoes the same reality when he writes about the man of lawlessness: *"Who opposes and exalts himself against every so-called god or object of worship, so that he takes his seat in the temple of God, proclaiming himself to be God." [2 Thess. 2:4 ESV]* Whether through a literal structure, a restored system, or a public act of sacrilege, Jesus points us to a visible, recognizable desecration. This will not be hidden ideology. It will be open defiance.

The urgency of this sign is unmistakable. Immediately after naming it, Jesus commands decisive action: *"Then let those who are in Judea flee to the mountains." [Matt. 24:16 NIV]* Delay becomes deadly. Hesitation becomes costly. The abomination is not merely theological—it is operational. It demands a response.

At the heart of this moment is a single question of authority. Who is worshiped? Who is obeyed? Who defines truth? The abomination demands allegiance. It replaces worship with coercion and devotion with control. This is why Jesus warns so soberly. What is at stake is not information, but loyalty.

By this point in the timeline, deception has reached its peak. Persecution has weakened resolve. The great falling away has thinned the faithful. Love has grown cold in many. Deception no longer whispers—it stands openly, just as it did in the days of Antiochus. Those who refused truth earlier will not recognize the moment. Those who loved truth will.

And yet, even here, God's mercy is still present. Warnings are issued. Time is allowed. An escape route is offered. Judgment never arrives without advance notice. The call is not to panic, but to discern and obey.

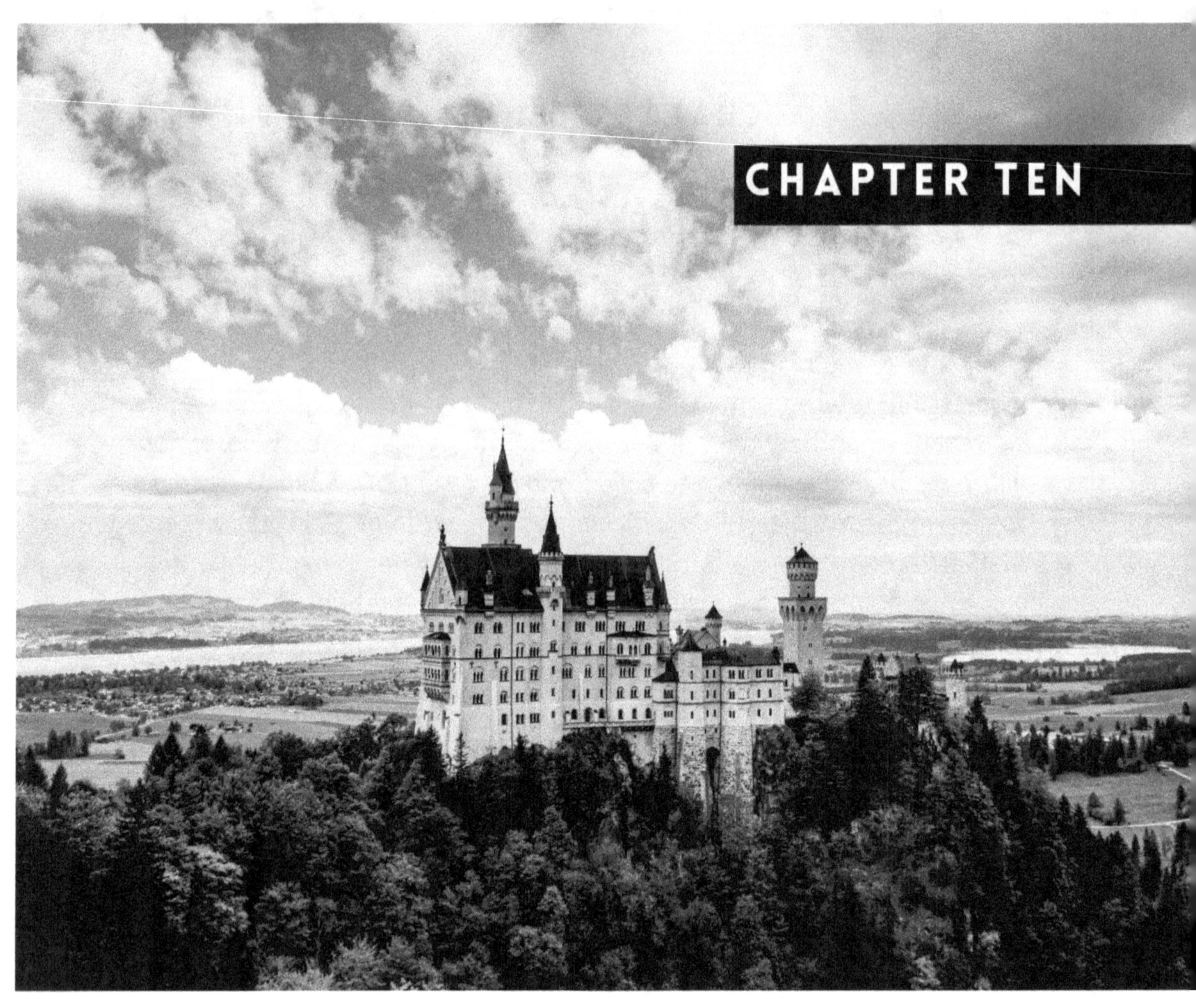

This moment marks a line in the sand that cannot be crossed. Before it, compromise may appear survivable. After it, allegiance becomes unmistakable. Neutrality disappears and silence becomes consent. Making a decision, at that moment, is unavoidable.

This is why Jesus says, "Let the reader understand." Understanding here is not intellectual agreement—it is obedient recognition. Just as the faithful recognized the abomination in 167 B.C., so the faithful will recognize it again. To see it and ignore it will be catastrophic but to recognize it and respond appropriately will be an act of faithfulness unto the end.

NEXT

THE ABOMINATION THAT CAUSES DESOLATION

Please read the scriptures, then answer the questions that follow.

ONE

MATTHEW 24:15-16 NIV

"So when you see standing in the holy place 'the abomination that causes desolation,' spoken of through the prophet Daniel—let the reader understand—then let those who are in Judea flee to the mountains."

TWO

DANIEL 9:27 NIV

"He will confirm a covenant with many for one 'seven.' In the middle of the 'seven' he will put an end to sacrifice and offering. And at the temple he will set up an abomination that causes desolation, until the end that is decreed is poured out on him.

THREE

DANIEL 11:31 NIV

"His armed forces will rise up to desecrate the temple fortress and will abolish the daily sacrifice. Then they will set up the abomination that causes desolation."

FOUR

DANIEL 12:11 NIV

"From the time that the daily sacrifice is abolished and the abomination that causes desolation is set up, there will be 1,290 days."

FIVE

MARK 13:14 NIV

"When you see 'the abomination that causes desolation' standing where it does not belong—let the reader understand—then let those who are in Judea flee to the mountains."

THE ABOMINATION THAT CAUSES DESOLATION

KEY SCRIPTURES

Please read the scriptures, then answer the questions that follow.

LUKE 21:20–22 NIV

"When you see Jerusalem being surrounded by armies, you will know that its desolation is near. Then let those who are in Judea flee to the mountains, let those in the city get out, and let those in the country not enter the city. For this is the time of punishment in fulfillment of all that has been written."

2 THESSALONIANS 2:3–4 NIV

"Don't let anyone deceive you in any way, for that day will not come until the rebellion occurs and the man of lawlessness is revealed, the man doomed to destruction. He will oppose and will exalt himself over everything that is called God or is worshiped, so that he sets himself up in God's temple, proclaiming himself to be God."

REVELATION 13:14–15 NIV

"Because of the signs it was given power to perform on behalf of the first beast, it deceived the inhabitants of the earth. It ordered them to set up an image in honor of the beast who was wounded by the sword and yet lived. The second beast was given power to give breath to the image of the first beast, so that the image could speak and cause all who refused to worship the image to be killed." (Read entire chapter for emphasis).

REVELATION 17:3 NIV

"Then the angel carried me away in the Spirit into a wilderness. There I saw a woman sitting on a scarlet beast that was covered with blasphemous names and had seven heads and ten horns." (Read entire chapter for emphasis).

HEBREWS 10:26–29 NIV

"If we deliberately keep on sinning after we have received the knowledge of the truth, no sacrifice for sins is left, but only a fearful expectation of judgment and of raging fire that will consume the enemies of God. Anyone who rejected the law of Moses died without mercy on the testimony of two or three witnesses. How much more severely do you think someone deserves to be punished who has trampled the Son of God underfoot, who has treated as an unholy thing the blood of the covenant that sanctified them, and who has insulted the Spirit of grace?"

NEXT

GROUP DISCUSSION QUESTIONS

CONSIDER THE SCRIPTURES READ, THEN ANSWER THE FOLLOWING QUESTIONS.

ASK YOURSELF...

Why does Jesus explicitly command readers to "understand" this sign? What does that imply about responsibility and discernment?

Why do you think Jesus deliberately connects His warning to Daniel's prophecy and a known historical fulfillment?

How does the historical fulfillment under Antiochus help us recognize future patterns?

Why are abominations always connected to false worship rather than merely immoral behavior?

What does Jesus's command to flee teach us about obedience versus spiritualizing danger away?

WRITE YOUR ANSWERS HERE....

NEXT

GROUP DISCUSSION QUESTIONS

CONSIDER THE SCRIPTURES READ, THEN ANSWER THE FOLLOWING QUESTIONS.

ASK YOURSELF...

WRITE YOUR ANSWERS HERE....

How does understanding the events of 167 B.C. sharpen our discernment for future deception?

Why is false worship—rather than political power alone—central to the abomination?

What does it mean practically that this sign requires immediate response, not delayed interpretation?

NEXT

Holy God,

You have told us that when what is holy is profaned,
desolation follows.
Sharpen our discernment. Strengthen our obedience.
Guard our hearts from compromise and our worship
from corruption.
Give us eyes to see what others overlook and
courage to respond when truth demands action. May
we recognize false authority, refuse counterfeit
worship, and remain faithful to You alone—to the
very end.
We choose allegiance over comfort, obedience over
delay,
and truth over survival. For there is no survival
outside of You.
In the name of Jesus Christ our Lord,
Amen.

CHAPTER 11
THE GREAT TRIBULATION

"For then there will be great tribulation, such as has not been from the beginning of the world until now—no, and never will be. And if those days had not been cut short, no human being would be saved. But for the sake of the elect those days will be cut short."

- Matthew 24:21-22 ESV

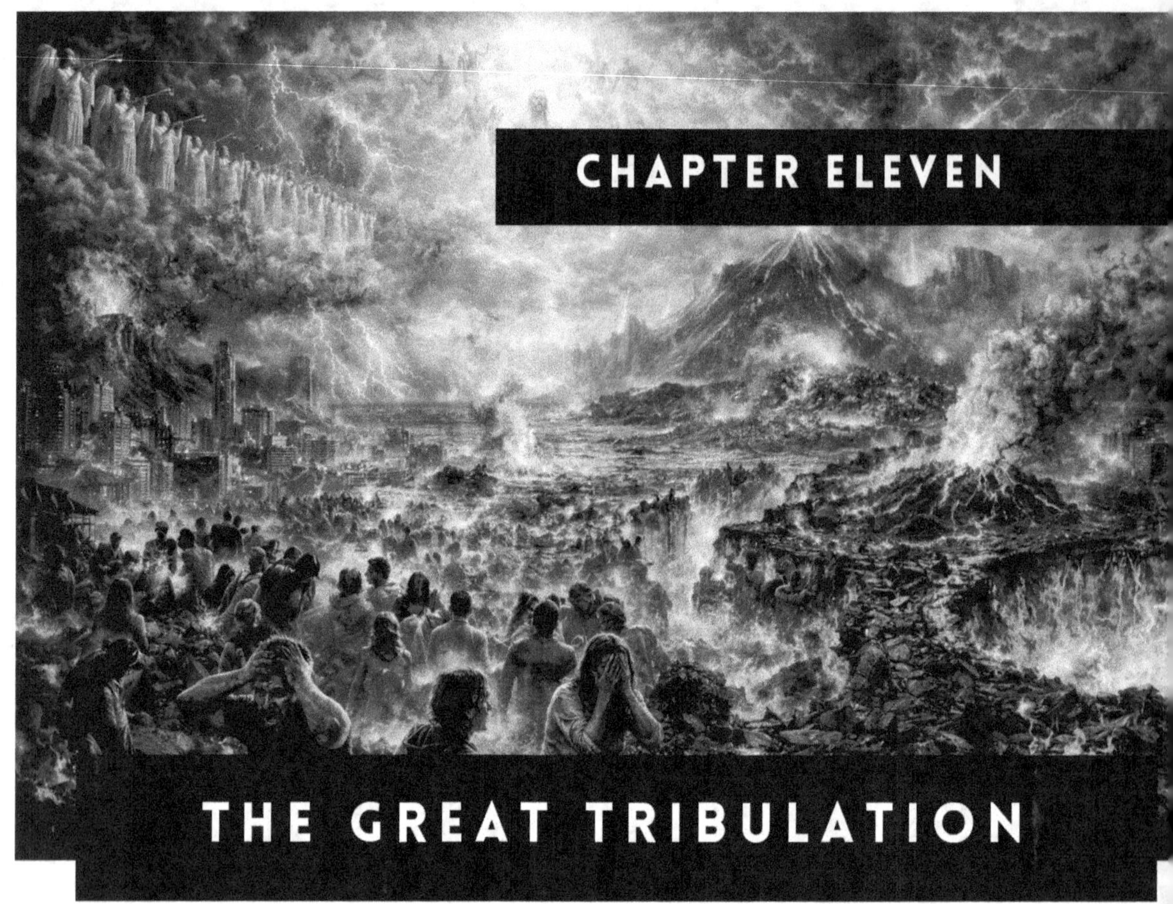

After teaching about the abomination that causes desolation, Jesus does not soften His words. He intensifies them. He names what follows with unmistakable gravity: the Great Tribulation. This is not a general season of difficulty, or the ordinary suffering that has marked human history. Jesus declares it to be unparalleled—a convergence of pressure, persecution, deception, and distress unlike anything the world has ever known or will ever know again. This is not hyperbole. It is divine warning.

The Great Tribulation is defined not only by suffering, but by the concentration of it. It is a time where evil accelerates, deception sharpens, and authority hardens. The consequences of rebellion converge all at once. What had been restrained now runs its course. Systems once moderated collapse into coercion. Truth is outlawed, allegiance is enforced, and survival itself becomes a test of faith. Jesus makes clear that this is not merely political upheaval or social unrest; it is spiritual conflict brought to its fiercest expression.

NEXT

THE GREAT TRIBULATION

"For then there will be great tribulation, such as has not been from the beginning of the world until now—no, and never will be. And if those days had not been cut short, no human being would be saved. But for the sake of the elect those days will be cut short."
—Matthew 24:21-22 ESV

Yet even in this darkest declaration, mercy breaks through. Jesus says something astonishing: "If those days had not been cut short, no human being would be saved." This reveals the severity of the hour—and the compassion of God. The shortening of the days is not arbitrary. It is intervention. It is restraint reintroduced at the brink of annihilation. God limits the duration of devastation for one reason alone: for the sake of the elect.

The elect are not spared because they are absent from the earth, but because they are preserved by God's faithfulness. The shortening of the days does not eliminate tribulation; it limits its reach. It ensures that endurance is possible. It guarantees that evil does not have the final word. Judgment is real, but it is never unchecked. Darkness advances only as far as God allows.

Jesus's words also correct a dangerous misunderstanding. The Great Tribulation is not evidence that God has abandoned His people. It is proof that He has not. If God were indifferent, there would be no limit. The very fact that the days are shortened testifies to covenant mercy. God remembers His promises even when the world appears unrecognizable.

This season tests more than strength—it tests allegiance. Comfort will be gone. Neutrality will be impossible. Our faith will no longer be theoretical. The question will not be whether one understands prophecy, but whether one trusts God when obedience costs everything. Endurance becomes the currency of faith. Those who belong to Christ are not called to conquer by force, but to overcome by faithfulness.

Jesus does not describe this moment to incite panic, but to anchor hope. The tribulation is great—but it is not endless. The days of tribulation are numbered. Its authority is limited. Its outcome is already determined. The shortening of the days point forward to a sudden interruption—not by relief, but by glory.

NEXT

THE GREAT TRIBULATION

The Great Tribulation is not the end of the story. It is the threshold. Beyond it lies the appearing of the Son of Man, the vindication of the faithful, and the restoration of all things. The darkness deepens—but only so that the light's arrival will be unmistakable.

For the believer, this truth steadies the heart. We do not measure faithfulness by ease, or interpret hardship as defeat. We remember that God governs time itself. Even the worst days are counted, and the fiercest trial is restrained. And even in the Great Tribulation, the Lord remains faithful to His own.

Therefore, hold fast and be strong in the Lord. The days are shortened for us who believe and the King is near.

"These are they who have come out of the great tribulation; they have washed their robes and made them white in the blood of the Lamb."
~ Revelation 7:14 NIV

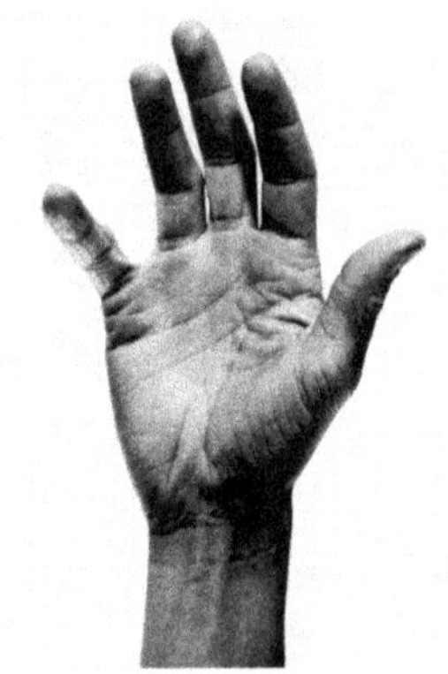

NEXT

THE GREAT TRIBULATION

KEY SCRIPTURES

Please read the scriptures, then answer the questions that follow.

ONE

MATTHEW 24:21-22 NIV

"For then there will be great distress, unequaled from the beginning of the world until now—and never to be equaled again. If those days had not been cut short, no one would survive, but for the sake of the elect those days will be shortened."

TWO

DANIEL 12:1 NIV

"At that time Michael, the great prince who protects your people, will arise. There will be a time of distress such as has not happened from the beginning of nations until then. But at that time your people—everyone whose name is found written in the book—will be delivered."

THREE

JEREMIAH 30:7 NIV

"How awful that day will be! No other will be like it. It will be a time of trouble for Jacob, but he will be saved out of it."

FOUR

REVELATION 7:14 NIV

"I answered, 'Sir, you know.' And he said, 'These are they who have come out of the great tribulation; they have washed their robes and made them white in the blood of the Lamb.'"

FIVE

REVELATION 6:9–11 NIV

"When he opened the fifth seal, I saw under the altar the souls of those who had been slain because of the word of God and the testimony they had maintained. They called out in a loud voice, 'How long, Sovereign Lord, holy and true, until you judge the inhabitants of the earth and avenge our blood?' Then each of them was given a white robe, and they were told to wait a little longer, until the full number of their fellow servants, their brothers and sisters, were killed just as they had been."

NEXT

THE GREAT TRIBULATION
KEY SCRIPTURES

Please read the scriptures, then answer the questions that follow.

ONE

REVELATION 13:5–7 NIV

"The beast was given a mouth to utter proud words and blasphemies and to exercise its authority for forty-two months. It opened its mouth to blaspheme God, and to slander his name and his dwelling place and those who live in heaven. It was given power to wage war against God's holy people and to conquer them. And it was given authority over every tribe, people, language and nation."

TWO

ISAIAH 54:9–10 NIV

"'To me this is like the days of Noah, when I swore that the waters of Noah would never again cover the earth. So now I have sworn not to be angry with you, never to rebuke you again. Though the mountains be shaken and the hills be removed, yet my unfailing love for you will not be shaken nor my covenant of peace be removed,' says the Lord, who has compassion on you."

THREE

ROMANS 8:18 NIV

"I consider that our present sufferings are not worth comparing with the glory that will be revealed in us."

FOUR

LAMENTATIONS 3:31–33 NIV

"For no one is cast off by the Lord forever. Though he brings grief, he will show compassion, so great is his unfailing love. For he does not willingly bring affliction or grief to anyone."

FIVE

HEBREWS 10:35–39 NIV

"So do not throw away your confidence; it will be richly rewarded. You need to persevere so that when you have done the will of God, you will receive what he has promised. For, 'In just a little while, he who is coming will come and will not delay.' And, 'But my righteous one will live by faith. And I take no pleasure in the one who shrinks back.' But we do not belong to those who shrink back and are destroyed, but to those who have faith and are saved."

NEXT

GROUP DISCUSSION QUESTIONS

CONSIDER THE SCRIPTURES READ, THEN ANSWER THE FOLLOWING QUESTIONS.

ASK YOURSELF...

WRITE YOUR ANSWERS HERE....

Why does Jesus describe the Great Tribulation as unmatched in all history? What does this reveal about its spiritual significance?

How does the shortening of the days reshape our understanding of God's mercy during judgment?

What does endurance look like practically when faith becomes costly?

How does knowing that tribulation is limited help guard believers against despair or panic?

Why is it important to distinguish between God's discipline, judgment, and covenant mercy during tribulation?

107

NEXT

Sovereign Lord,
You warned us of days unlike any the world
has known in order to anchor us.
You remind us that even the darkest hours are counted,
and even great tribulation is restrained by Your mercy.
Strengthen our endurance. Stabilize our hearts.
Teach us to trust You when comfort disappears and faith
becomes costly.
Help us to stand firm, not shrinking back,
to endure faithfully, not fearfully,
and to hope confidently, knowing You govern time itself.
Give us endurance when comfort disappears.
Give us courage when neutrality is impossible,
and hope when obedience costs everything.
Thank You that even the darkest days are numbered,
that evil is restrained by Your hand,
and that glory waits beyond the trial.
Teach us to trust You—not because the days are easy,
but because they are numbered.
We hold fast to you
because You are faithful.
And You will finish what You began.
In the name of our Lord Jesus Christ,
Amen.

CHAPTER 12
THE TWO WITNESSES

"And I will appoint my two witnesses, and they will prophesy for 1,260 days, clothed in sackcloth."

—Revelation 11:3 NIV

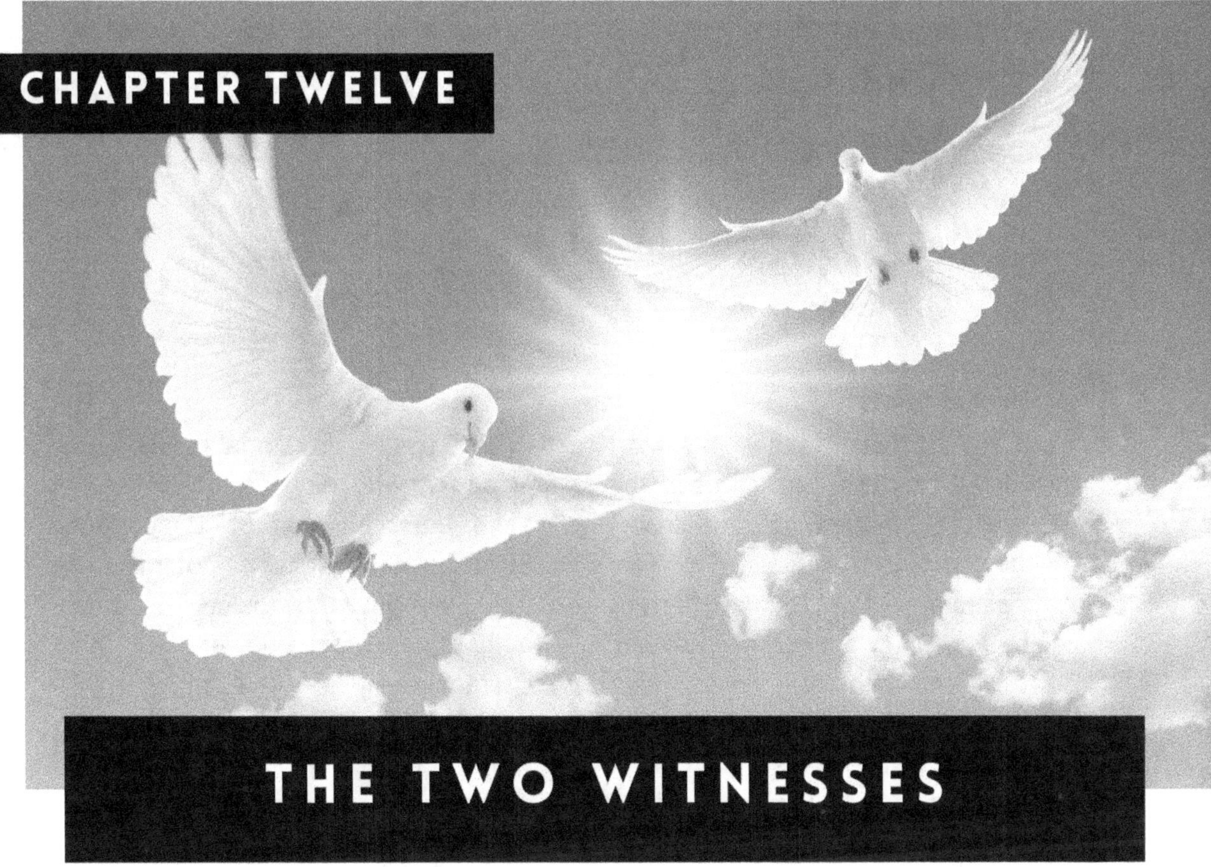

THE TWO WITNESSES

As darkness intensifies and deception consolidates its grip on the world, God does something unmistakable and deliberate. He sends witnesses—not arguments, institutions, philosophers or political movements. He sends living testimony. The Two Witnesses appear at the height of global resistance to truth —not before persecution, not after tribulation, but squarely in the middle of it. This reveals something essential about God's character: judgment never arrives without testimony, and exposure never comes without warning.

Scripture is precise in naming two witnesses, because God operates according to His own standard. *"Every matter must be established by the testimony of two or three witnesses." [Deuteronomy 19:15 CSB]* What unfolds in Revelation is not symbolic rumor or mystical suggestion. It is legally sufficient, spiritually authoritative, and publicly undeniable testimony. What the witnesses proclaim is not opinion. It is an indictment and an invitation—truth spoken plainly before the world.

NEXT

THE TWO WITNESSES

"And I will appoint my two witnesses, and they will prophesy for 1,260 days, clothed in sackcloth."
~ Revelation 11:3 NIV

They are clothed in sackcloth, and this detail matters. Sackcloth is the garment of mourning, repentance, urgency, and grief over sin. The Two Witnesses do not arrive triumphant or celebratory. They arrive grieving. They do not entertain the world; they confront it. Their message is not softened to fit the times. They speak as prophets, not diplomats, carrying the weight of heaven's sorrow over human rebellion.

Their assignment is measured precisely: 1,260 days—three and a half years. This period echoes throughout Scripture as a time of intense testing, limited evil authority, and measured judgment. Evil is active, but it is restrained. God is patient, but He is precise. The clock is not symbolic. It is intentional. Nothing in this moment is random or uncontrolled.

Revelation describes their authority in language that cannot be ignored. Fire proceeds from their mouths. The sky is shut so that no rain falls. The earth is struck with plagues. These signs echo the ministries of Moses and Elijah, but Scripture does not insist on their identities. It insists on their authority. Their power is not spectacle—it is resistance and confirmation that God sent them. The world does not ignore them because it cannot.

The hatred they provoke is immediate and intense. Revelation tells us that when they are finally killed, *"the inhabitants of the earth will gloat over them and celebrate their deaths." [Rev. 11:10 NIV]* The celebration is revealing. The truth of their existence afflicts deception. Their light tortures the darkness. The exposure of their assignment torments systems built on lies. The world does not reject the witnesses because it fails to understand them. It rejects them because it understands exactly what they represent.

Their deaths, however, are not

NEXT

THE TWO WITNESSES

accidental or premature. They are not killed until their testimony is finished, their assignment is complete, and God permits it. *"When they have finished their testimony, the beast… will kill them."* [Rev. 11:7 NIV] Evil does not interrupt God's plan. It operates within boundaries it cannot cross.

Their bodies are left exposed in public humiliation. There's no burial, no honor, and no dignity. The world watches—and rejoices. Technology becomes the instrument of mockery as their deaths are broadcast and celebrated. The world believes it has finally silenced truth. This moment is not incidental. It is prophetic. It reveals the depth of hatred toward God's testimony.

Then the celebration ends. *"After three and a half days, the breath of life from God entered them."* [Rev. 11:11] There is no secrecy and no metaphor. Resurrection happens in plain sight. Fear replaces their celebration. Shock replaces their mockery and God has the final word.

A loud voice from heaven calls them upward. They ascend as their enemies watch. Immediately, the earth responds. An earthquake strikes. A tenth of the city collapses. Thousands of people are killed in the earthquake. Survivors are terrified—and some give glory to God. Even here, repentance flickers. Mercy has not yet fully withdrawn.

The Two Witnesses reveal truths the world cannot escape. God's mercy endures until the very end. Truth will be spoken publicly, not privately. Evil will be exposed openly. Death does not defeat testimony. Their ministry stands as God's final, unmistakable declaration to humanity: you were warned, you were told, and you were given opportunity. Therefore, there are no acceptable excuses.

For the faithful, the Two Witnesses confirm something vital. God does not ask His people to endure in silence without support. He bears witness Himself. Their ministry assures believers that they are not forgotten, not mistaken, and not alone. Truth may be hated, but it will not be silenced.

NEXT

THE TWO WITNESSES

KEY SCRIPTURES

Please read the scriptures, then answer the questions that follow.

ONE

REVELATION 11:3-6 NIV

"'And I will appoint my two witnesses, and they will prophesy for 1,260 days, clothed in sackcloth.' They are 'the two olive trees' and the two lampstands, and 'they stand before the Lord of the earth.' If anyone tries to harm them, fire comes from their mouths and devours their enemies. This is how anyone who wants to harm them must die. They have power to shut up the heavens so that it will not rain during the time they are prophesying; and they have power to turn the waters into blood and to strike the earth with every kind of plague as often as they want."

TWO

ZECHARIAH 4:11-14 NIV

"Then I asked the angel, 'What are these two olive trees on the right and the left of the lampstand?' Again I asked him, 'What are these two olive branches beside the two gold pipes that pour out golden oil?' He replied, 'Do you not know what these are?' 'No, my lord,' I said. So he said, 'These are the two who are anointed to serve the Lord of all the earth.'"

THREE

MALACHI 4:5-6 NIV

"See, I will send the prophet Elijah to you before that great and dreadful day of the Lord comes. He will turn the hearts of the parents to their children, and the hearts of the children to their parents; or else I will come and strike the land with total destruction."

FOUR

JOHN 15:18–20 NIV

"If the world hates you, keep in mind that it hated me first. If you belonged to the world, it would love you as its own. As it is, you do not belong to the world, but I have chosen you out of the world. That is why the world hates you. Remember what I told you: 'A servant is not greater than his master.' If they persecuted me, they will persecute you also. If they obeyed my teaching, they will obey yours also."

FIVE

REVELATION 12:11 NIV

"They triumphed over him by the blood of the Lamb and by the word of their testimony; they did not love their lives so much as to shrink from death."

NEXT

GROUP DISCUSSION QUESTIONS

CONSIDER THE SCRIPTURES READ, THEN ANSWER THE FOLLOWING QUESTIONS.

Why does God send witnesses in the middle of tribulation instead of arguments or institutions in the final hour? What does this reveal about how God confronts deception?

1

What does the sackcloth imagery teach us about the tone and posture of true witness? What does it reveal about God's heart toward a rebellious world?

2

Why does the world celebrate the death of the witnesses? What does that reveal about humanity's relationship to truth?

3

How does the public resurrection of the witnesses strengthen the faith of believers living under persecution?

4

NEXT

Prayer

Faithful God,

You have never left the world without a witness.
Even in the darkest hour, You appoint testimony
that cannot be silenced.
Give us hearts that grieve over sin,
voices that proclaim Your truth,
and endurance that trusts You with the outcome.
When fear rises, remind us that death does not
silence truth.
When opposition intensifies, anchor us in
obedience.
As You send witnesses in the darkest hour,
make us faithful witnesses where You have placed
us.
May we speak, stand, and endure—
trusting that resurrection belongs to You.
We choose to bear witness—
not for applause, or for survival,
but for Your glory.
In the mighty name of Jesus Christ we pray,

Amen.

NEXT

CHAPTER 13
THE SUN DARKENED AND THE HEAVENS SHAKEN

NEXT

"Immediately after the distress of those days, 'the sun will be darkened, and the moon will not give its light; the stars will fall from the sky, and the heavenly bodies will be shaken.'"

—MATTHEW 24:29 NIV

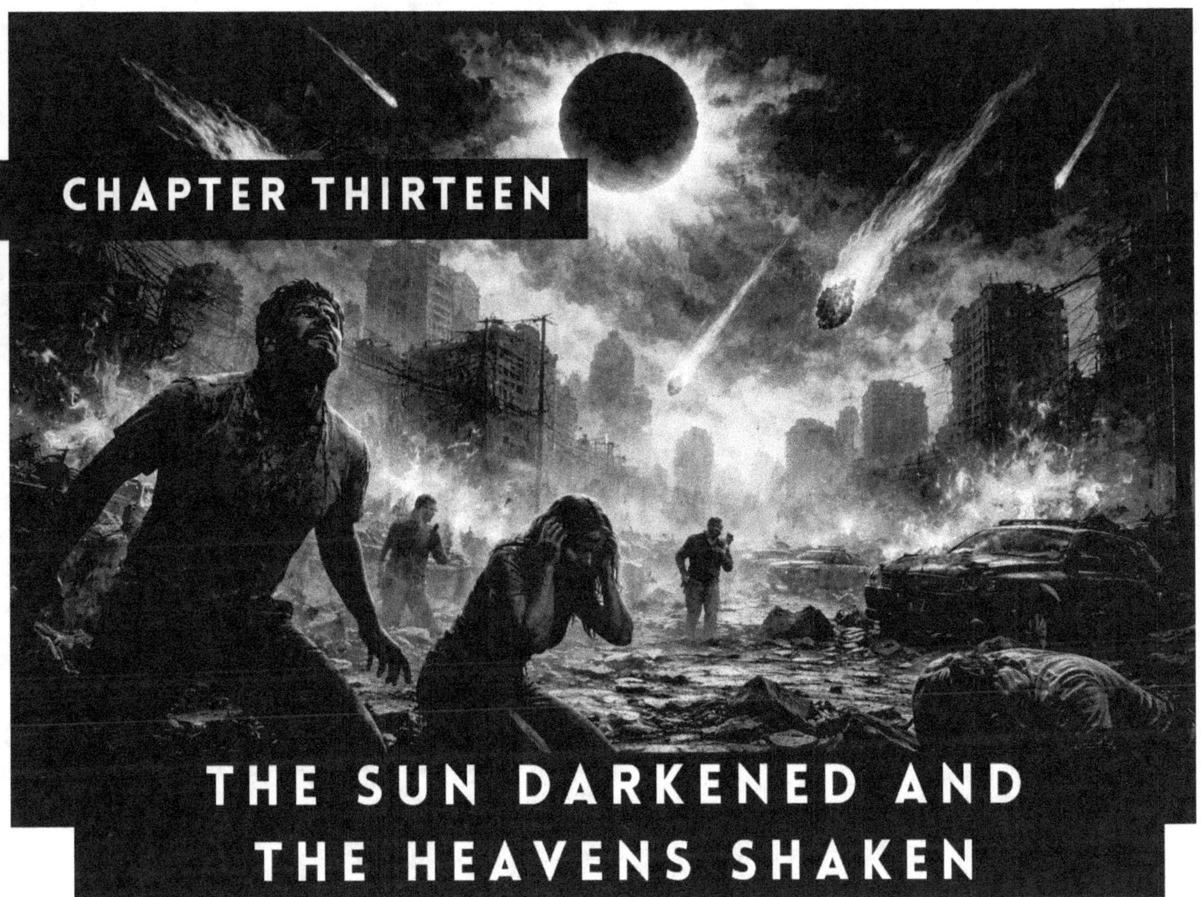

CHAPTER THIRTEEN

THE SUN DARKENED AND THE HEAVENS SHAKEN

Jesus marks this moment with unmistakable precision: immediately after the distress of those days. It's not a gradual progression. It is not symbolical and is not done in secret. Heaven interrupts history. What has been unfolding within human systems now breaks beyond them. The stage is no longer confined to earth. The sky itself becomes a sign. Creation, long groaning under the weight of rebellion, now speaks with a voice that cannot be silenced.

Throughout the Bible, heavenly disturbance signals decisive, divine intervention. When God acts in final authority, creation responds, the heavens bear witness, and human power is reduced to its proper scale. Joel foretold it plainly: *"The sun will be turned to darkness and the moon to blood before the coming of the great and dreadful day of the Lord."* [Joel 2:31 NIV] These are not metaphors meant to be explained away. They are announcements meant to be recognized. When the heavens move, God is declaring that history has reached its appointed threshold.

The darkening of the sun and moon strikes at the illusion of human control. These lights govern time, seasons, and the rhythms of daily life. When they fail, normalcy collapses; predictability dissolves, and control evaporates.   The systems

119

THE SUN DARKENED AND THE HEAVENS SHAKEN

"Immediately after the distress of those days, 'the sun will be darkened, and the moon will not give its light; the stars will fall from the sky, and the heavenly bodies will be shaken.'" —Matthew 24:29 NIV

humanity relies upon—economies, calendars, schedules, power grids, and forecasts—lose their anchor. This is not chaos for chaos' sake. It is exposure. Creation reveals that it never belonged to humanity. It belongs to God.

Jesus goes further. He declares that the heavenly bodies themselves will be shaken. This is not merely atmospheric disturbance; it is heavenly reckoning. The author of Hebrews interprets this shaking with clarity: *"The words 'once more' indicate the removing of what can be shaken—that is, created things—so that what cannot be shaken may remain."* [Heb. 12:27 NIV] Shaking is selective. What is temporary collapses, but what is eternal stands. God is not destroying creation at random; He is separating what endures from what cannot.

The timing of these signs matters. They do not precede deception and do not accompany rumors or speculation. They follow endurance.

By this point, testimony has been given, allegiance has been revealed, and mercy has been extended. The witnesses have spoken. The faithful have endured. The rebellious have chosen. Now the universe itself testifies that the age is ending. The heavens announce what humanity can no longer deny.

Up to this moment, people can debate causes. They can assign blame, control narratives, and argue interpretations, but when the heavens respond, plausible denial collapses. Revelation describes the response with terrifying honesty: "People hid in caves… and called to the mountains, *'Fall on us!'"* [Rev 6:16 NIV] In this moment fear will replace denial. There will no longer be a need for explanation. Reckoning will enter like a wrecking ball. No argument will remain when the sky itself bears witness.

The Word is clear about what these signs are not. They are not random astronomical anomalies, natural

THE SUN DARKENED AND THE HEAVENS SHAKEN

cycles, or merely human-induced effects. They are intentional acts of God. They do not point only to human failure; they announce divine arrival. The Creator steps forward, and creation responds.

Before Christ appears, creation delivers its final message. The heavens declare that the age is closing, judgment is near, and authority is shifting. Just as a trumpet announces a king, the sky announces the coming of the Son of Man. The universe becomes the herald of His return.

Jesus had already prepared His disciples for this moment. *"When these things begin to take place, stand up and lift up your heads, because your redemption is drawing near."* [Luke 21:28 NIV] What terrifies the rebellious steadies the faithful. The same signs that cause panic in the world produce hope in those who belong to Christ. This is not bravado. It is recognition.

The shaking of the heavens presses a question no one can avoid. When everything familiar disappears, what remains? Only what is anchored in Jesus survives.

"The heavens declare the glory of God; the skies proclaim the work of his hands."
~ Psalm 19:1 NIV

THE SUN DARKENED AND THE HEAVENS SHAKEN

KEY SCRIPTURES

Please read the scriptures, then answer the questions that follow.

ONE

MATTHEW 24:29 NIV

"Immediately after the distress of those days 'the sun will be darkened, and the moon will not give its light; the stars will fall from the sky, and the heavenly bodies will be shaken.'"

TWO

JOEL 2:30–31 NIV

"I will show wonders in the heavens and on the earth, blood and fire and billows of smoke. The sun will be turned to darkness and the moon to blood before the coming of the great and dreadful day of the Lord."

THREE

ISAIAH 13:9–11 NIV

"See, the day of the Lord is coming—a cruel day, with wrath and fierce anger—to make the land desolate and destroy the sinners within it. The stars of heaven and their constellations will not show their light. The rising sun will be darkened and the moon will not give its light. I will punish the world for its evil, the wicked for their sins. I will put an end to the arrogance of the haughty and will humble the pride of the ruthless."

FOUR

HEBREWS 12:26–27 NIV

"At that time his voice shook the earth, but now he has promised, 'Once more I will shake not only the earth but also the heavens.' The words 'once more' indicate the removing of what can be shaken—that is, created things—so that what cannot be shaken may remain."

FIVE

PSALM 102:25–27 NIV

"In the beginning you laid the foundations of the earth, and the heavens are the work of your hands. They will perish, but you remain; they will all wear out like a garment. Like clothing you will change them and they will be discarded. But you remain the same, and your years will never end."

NEXT

THE SUN DARKENED AND THE HEAVENS SHAKEN

KEY SCRIPTURES

Please read the scriptures, then answer the questions that follow.

ONE

HAGGAI 2:6–7 NIV

"This is what the Lord Almighty says: 'In a little while I will once more shake the heavens and the earth, the sea and the dry land. I will shake all nations, and what is desired by all nations will come, and I will fill this house with glory,' says the Lord Almighty."

TWO

PSALM 19:1 NIV

"The heavens declare the glory of God; the skies proclaim the work of his hands."

THREE

LUKE 21:25–28 NIV

"There will be signs in the sun, moon and stars. On the earth, nations will be in anguish and perplexity at the roaring and tossing of the sea. People will faint from terror, apprehensive of what is coming on the world, for the heavenly bodies will be shaken. At that time they will see the Son of Man coming in a cloud with power and great glory. When these things begin to take place, stand up and lift up your heads, because your redemption is drawing near."

FOUR

ACTS 2:20 NIV

"The sun will be turned to darkness and the moon to blood before the coming of the great and glorious day of the Lord."

FIVE

REVELATION 6:12–14 NIV

"I watched as he opened the sixth seal. There was a great earthquake. The sun turned black like sackcloth made of goat hair, the whole moon turned blood red, and the stars in the sky fell to earth, as figs drop from a fig tree when shaken by a strong wind. The heavens receded like a scroll being rolled up, and every mountain and island was removed from its place." (Read entire chapter)

NEXT

GROUP DISCUSSION QUESTIONS

CONSIDER THE SCRIPTURES READ, THEN ANSWER THE FOLLOWING QUESTIONS.

ASK YOURSELF...	WRITE YOUR ANSWERS HERE....
Why does Jesus emphasize that these signs occur after the tribulation rather than before it? What does this say about God's order and mercy?	
How does the shaking of the heavens expose the illusion of human control?	
Why do these signs produce terror in some and hope in others? What makes the difference?	
What does it mean to live anchored in what "cannot be shaken" right now?	
What does Hebrews 12 teach us about why God shakes what can be shaken?	

NEXT

Sovereign God,
You shake the heavens to reveal who is in control.
When the lights we trust go dark
and the familiar dissolves,
we are reminded that You remain unshaken.
We declare Your kingdom.
We are assured that Your hand protects us through
the shaking.
We stand firm when the world trembles
and lift our heads with confidence
as redemption draws near.
May our lives testify to Your glory
until the Son of Man appears.
In the name of Jesus Christ our Lord we pray,
Amen.

CHAPTER 14
THE RAPTURE

NEXT

"**And He will send His angels with a loud trumpet call, and they will gather His elect from the four winds, from one end of the heavens to the other.**"
—**Matthew 24:31 NIV**

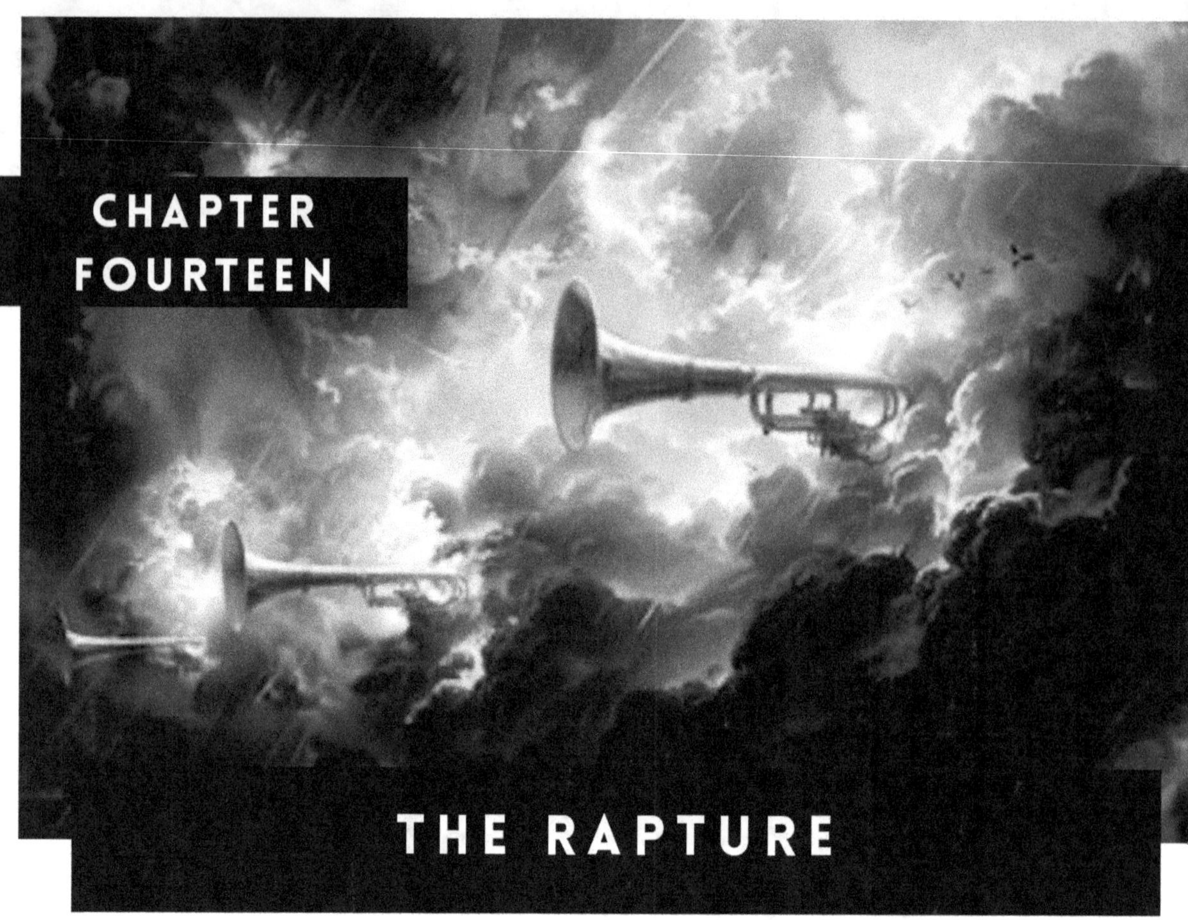

THE RAPTURE

The return of Christ will not slip quietly into history. It will be announced. Jesus says there will be a loud trumpet call—a sound that ends waiting and shatters delay. In Scripture, trumpets are never background noise. They announce the arrival of a King, the issuing of a divine command, and a moment that demands response. This trumpet does not invite discussion or negotiation. It summons.

There is a reason God chooses a trumpet. Throughout the Bible, trumpets mark sacred thresholds: the assembly of God's people, the movement of Israel through the wilderness, the manifestation of God's presence, and the declaration of victory. Paul ties this moment together with unmistakable clarity when he writes, *"For the Lord himself will descend from heaven with a cry of command, with the voice of an archangel, and with the sound of the trumpet of God. And the dead in Christ will rise first. Then we who are alive, who are left, will be caught up together with them in the clouds to meet the Lord in the air, and so we will always be with the Lord." [1 Thess. 4:16 ESV]* The trumpet signals completion. What was promised across generations is finally fulfilled.

NEXT

THE RAPTURE

"And He will send His angels with a loud trumpet call, and they will gather His elect from the four winds, from one end of the heavens to the other."
—Matthew 24:31 NIV

Jesus names those who respond as the elect. This is not an elite class defined by visibility, influence, or earthly success. The elect are those chosen by God, known to Him, and faithful to Him. They are the ones who endured persecution without denying His name, resisted deception when lies were rewarded, and held fast under pressure when compromise seemed easier. Election here is not favoritism; it is relationship. God gathers those who belong to Him.

The scope of this gathering leaves no room for doubt. Jesus says they are gathered from the four winds—north, south, east, and west—from one end of the heavens to the other. This is not a regional event or a partial rescue. It is a global gathering. Every hidden believer, every silenced witness, every faithful soul whose obedience went unseen by the world is known to God. None are forgotten or overlooked.

Jesus makes clear that this gathering is not accomplished by human effort. He sends His angels. This is divine action from beginning to end. The same heavenly beings who carried God's messages, executed His judgments, and guarded His purposes now perform a final act of mercy. They gather. God does not outsource redemption. He completes it Himself.

Scripture connects this gathering directly to resurrection. Paul explains that *"the dead in Christ will rise first,"* and that we who are still alive will be caught up together with them. *[1 Thess. 4:16–17 NIV]* This is not an escape from responsibility; it is the restoration of what was lost. Families are reunited, faith is vindicated, and death is defeated. What sin scattered, Christ regathers.

Nothing about this moment is hidden. The trumpet is loud. The angels are visible. The gathering is global. Jesus describes a public, unmistakable event that follows heavenly signs and His visible return. What God completes, He does openly.

Paul tells the Church that these words are meant to comfort. *"Therefore encourage one another with these words." [1 Thess. 4:18 NIV]* Comfort

NEXT

THE RAPTURE

is needed because endurance is often lonely, faithfulness is often costly, and obedience is rarely rewarded immediately. This gathering declares a final truth that silences every doubt: nothing faithful was wasted.

From Eden onward, humanity has lived in scattering—by sin, by exile, or by death. This moment reverses it all. God gathers His people not by geography, not by nationality, and not by status, but by allegiance. The Shepherd calls and the sheep respond.

The trumpet will sound for everyone. But it gathers only those who belong to Christ. The question is not whether you will hear it. The question is whether it will be a summons—or a warning.

"The Sovereign Lord will sound the trumpet; he will march in the storms of the south."
~ Zechariah 9:14b NIV

NEXT

THE RAPTURE

KEY SCRIPTURES

Please read the scriptures, then answer the questions that follow.

ONE

1 CORINTHIANS 15:51–52 NIV

"Listen, I tell you a mystery: We will not all sleep, but we will all be changed—in a flash, in the twinkling of an eye, at the last trumpet. For the trumpet will sound, the dead will be raised imperishable, and we will be changed."

TWO

1 THESSALONIANS 4:16–18 NIV

"For the Lord himself will come down from heaven, with a loud command, with the voice of the archangel and with the trumpet call of God, and the dead in Christ will rise first. After that, we who are still alive and are left will be caught up together with them in the clouds to meet the Lord in the air. And so we will be with the Lord forever. Therefore encourage one another with these words."

THREE

HEBREWS 9:28 NIV

"So Christ was sacrificed once to take away the sins of many; and he will appear a second time, not to bear sin, but to bring salvation to those who are waiting for him."

FOUR

REVELATION 7:9–10 NIV

"After this I looked, and there before me was a great multitude that no one could count, from every nation, tribe, people and language, standing before the throne and before the Lamb. They were wearing white robes and were holding palm branches in their hands. And they cried out in a loud voice: 'Salvation belongs to our God, who sits on the throne, and to the Lamb.'"

FIVE

REVELATION 14:14–16 NIV

"I looked, and there before me was a white cloud, and seated on the cloud was one like a son of man with a crown of gold on his head and a sharp sickle in his hand. Then another angel came out of the temple and called in a loud voice to him who was sitting on the cloud, 'Take your sickle and reap, because the time to reap has come, for the harvest of the earth is ripe.' So he who was seated on the cloud swung his sickle over the earth, and the earth was harvested."

NEXT

GROUP DISCUSSION QUESTIONS

CONSIDER THE SCRIPTURES READ, THEN ANSWER THE FOLLOWING QUESTIONS.

ONE
Why does Scripture consistently use trumpets to announce God's decisive actions? What does that tell us about the nature of Christ's return?

TWO
How does the public nature of the gathering challenge ideas of secrecy or private removal?

THREE
Read John 10:27-28. Based on this, what defines the "elect" according to Jesus's teaching—not theologically, but practically?

FOUR
How does the promise of resurrection and reunion strengthen endurance now?

FIVE
Why does Scripture emphasize that the trumpet is loud and unmistakable?

SIX
How does understanding the gathering as restoration reshape common ideas about escape or avoidance?

SEVEN
How should the promise of resurrection and gathering shape the way believers endure hardship now?

NEXT

# Prayer

Sovereign God,
You promised that the waiting would end
and that Your people would be gathered.
Strengthen our endurance as we wait.
Anchor our hope in resurrection and
keep our hearts ready.
Teach us to live now
as those who belong to You—
listening for Your voice,
holding fast through pressure,
and trusting that nothing faithful is forgotten.
When the trumpet sounds,
we want to go home to live with You.
Until that day, we watch. We wait. We belong to You.
In the mighty name of Jesus we pray,
Amen.

CHAPTER 15
THE LEFT BEHIND ERA: ONE TAKEN, ONE LEFT

"Two men will be in the field; one will be taken and the other left. Two women will be grinding with a hand mill; one will be taken and the other left."

—Matthew 24:40–41 NIV

THE LEFT BEHIND ERA: ONE TAKEN, ONE LEFT

Few sayings of Jesus have been more quoted than this one. *One taken and one left.* What Jesus is describing is not randomness. It is separation. Two people stand side by side, engaged in the same labor, sharing the same space and routine. One is taken, and the other is left. Geography does not decide this moment. Proximity does not protect. This separation is not about where you stand, but who you belong to. Closeness to believers does not equal allegiance to Christ. Familiarity with faith does not equal obedience.

Jesus anchors this warning in history by pointing to the days of Noah. *"As it was in the days of Noah, so it will be at the coming of the Son of Man."* [Matt. 24:37 NIV] In Noah's generation, life continued as usual. People married, worked, planned, and dismissed warnings. The ark stood in plain sight and Noah's preaching continued, then separation came suddenly. And it is here that Jesus's comparison becomes unsettling. Those who were taken away by the flood were not the righteous. They were the unprepared. The righteous were preserved. This forces an uncomfortable but necessary question: In Jesus's words, who is being taken, and who is being left?

NEXT

THE LEFT BEHIND ERA: ONE TAKEN, ONE LEFT

"Two men will be in the field; one will be taken and the other left. Two women will be grinding with a hand mill; one will be taken and the other left."
—Matthew 24:40–41 NIV

The flood narrative clarifies the tension. The righteous were left alive. The unrighteous were swept away. Jesus's language deliberately echoes this pattern. The emphasis is not on escape, but on readiness. The issue is not movement, but preparation. What matters is not whether you are near the people of God, but whether you have responded to the call of God.

Jesus underscores this warning by emphasizing ordinary life. People are working fields. Women are grinding grain. Daily labor continues uninterrupted. Why does Jesus highlight the mundane? Because the greatest danger is not chaos, but normalcy without discernment. The last days are not marked only by terror and upheaval. They are marked by people carrying on as usual, dismissing the urgency of repentance while time still remains.

Proximity does not protect. Standing next to a believer will not save anyone. Faith cannot be borrowed. Readiness cannot be inherited. Obedience cannot be outsourced. This is the most painful reality of separation. Families are divided. Friends are separated. Communities are fractured—not by violence, but by allegiance. What was once shared outwardly is revealed inwardly to be different.

It is no accident that Jesus follows this teaching immediately with a command to watchfulness. *"Therefore keep watch, because you do not know on what day your Lord will come."* [Matt. 24:42 NIV] Watchfulness is not anxiety. It is active faithfulness. Those who are watching are not surprised but those who drift are.

The so-called "left behind" moment is not about spectacle or sensational fear. It is about revelation. It reveals who endured, who compromised, who truly believed in Christ, and who merely associated with Him. Separation does not create difference. It exposes what was already there.

This warning cuts especially close to those inside religious spaces. Church attendance is not readiness. Religious

137

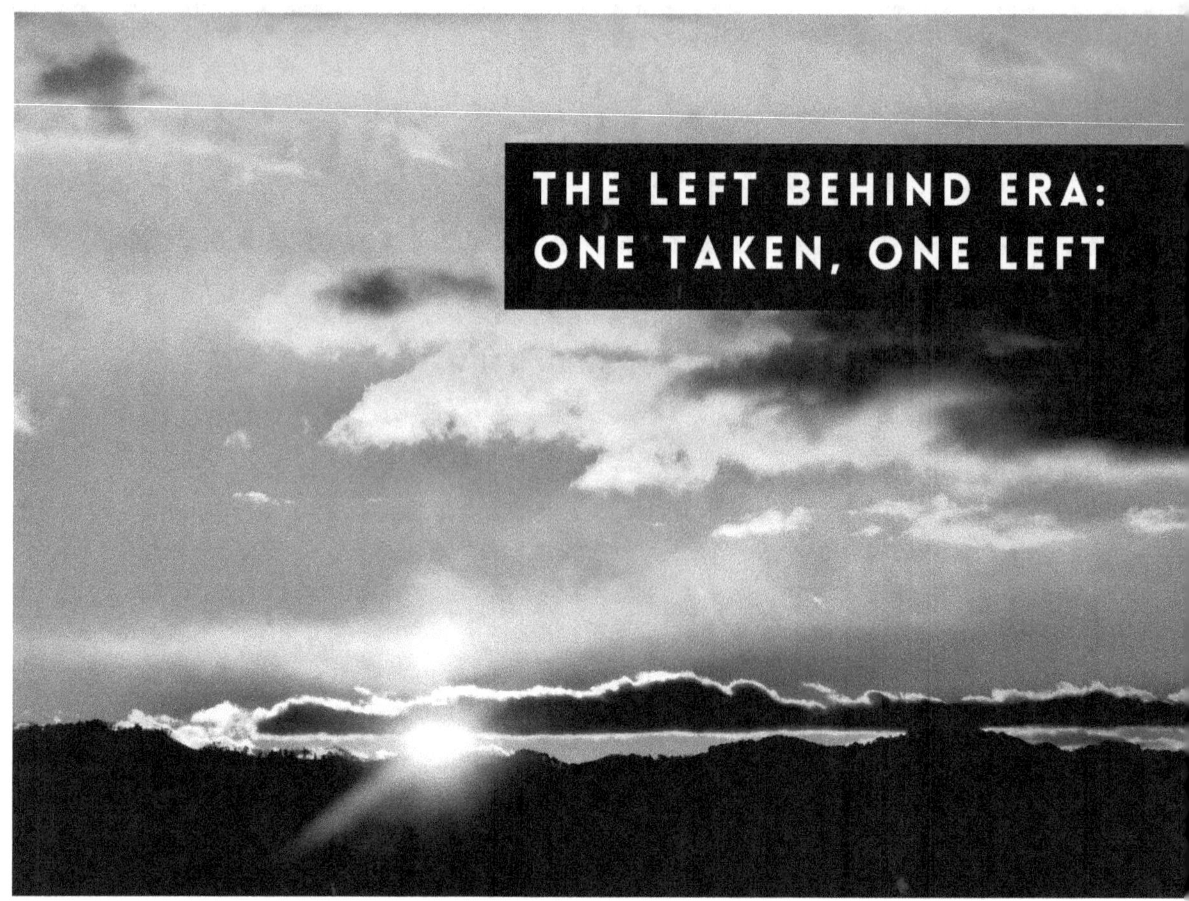

language is not allegiance. Quoting scripture is not obedience. Jesus warned plainly, *"Not everyone who says to Me, 'Lord, Lord,' will enter the kingdom of heaven"* [Matt 7:21 NIV] Association is not surrender.

For the faithful, however, this moment is not terror. It is confirmation. The King knows His own. Faithfulness that went unseen, unrewarded, or misunderstood is now revealed. What was costly is now vindicated.

Jesus does not ask which group you would prefer to be in. He asks something far more piercing: Are you ready? Because when separation comes, preparation has already been decided.

KEY TAKEAWAYS

- Be watchful
- Be obedient to Christ
- Recognize the signs of the times
- Encourage other believers of Christ's Return.

NEXT

KEY SCRIPTURES

Please read the scriptures, then answer the questions that follow.

ONE

MATTHEW 24:42-44 NIV

"Therefore keep watch, because you do not know on what day your Lord will come. But understand this: If the owner of the house had known at what time of night the thief was coming, he would have kept watch and would not have let his house be broken into. So you also must be ready, because the Son of Man will come at an hour when you do not expect him."

TWO

GENESIS 7:21–23 NIV

"Every living thing that moved on land perished—birds, livestock, wild animals, all the creatures that swarm over the earth, and all mankind. Everything on dry land that had the breath of life in its nostrils died. Every living thing on the face of the earth was wiped out; people and animals and the creatures that move along the ground and the birds were wiped from the earth. Only Noah was left, and those with him in the ark."

THREE

LUKE 17:26-29 NIV (ALSO READ VERSES 30-33)

"Just as it was in the days of Noah, so also will it be in the days of the Son of Man. People were eating, drinking, marrying and being given in marriage up to the day Noah entered the ark. Then the flood came and destroyed them all. It was the same in the days of Lot. People were eating and drinking, buying and selling, planting and building. But the day Lot left Sodom, fire and sulfur rained down from heaven and destroyed them all."

FOUR

MATTHEW 7:21-23 NIV

"Not everyone who says to me, 'Lord, Lord,' will enter the kingdom of heaven, but only the one who does the will of my Father who is in heaven. Many will say to me on that day, 'Lord, Lord, did we not prophesy in your name and in your name drive out demons and in your name perform many miracles?' Then I will tell them plainly, 'I never knew you. Away from me, you evildoers!'"

FIVE

MATTHEW 25:1-5 NIV

"At that time the kingdom of heaven will be like ten virgins who took their lamps and went out to meet the bridegroom. Five of them were foolish and five were wise. The foolish ones took their lamps but did not take any oil with them. The wise ones, however, took oil in jars along with their lamps. The bridegroom was a long time in coming, and they all became drowsy and fell asleep."

NEXT

KEY SCRIPTURES

Please read the scriptures, then answer the questions that follow.

ONE

MATTHEW 24:36-37, 39 NIV

"But about that day or hour no one knows, not even the angels in heaven, nor the Son, but only the Father. As it was in the days of Noah, so it will be at the coming of the Son of Man. And they knew nothing about what would happen until the flood came and took them all away. That is how it will be at the coming of the Son of Man."

TWO

2 CORINTHIANS 13:5 NIV

"Examine yourselves to see whether you are in the faith; test yourselves. Do you not realize that Christ Jesus is in you—unless, of course, you fail the test?"

THREE

HEBREWS 3:14 NIV

"We have come to share in Christ, if indeed we hold our original conviction firmly to the very end."

FOUR

1 PETER 1:17 NIV

"Since you call on a Father who judges each person's work impartially, live out your time as foreigners here in reverent fear."

FIVE

AMOS 3:2 NIV

"You only have I chosen of all the families of the earth; therefore I will punish you for all your sins."

NEXT

GROUP DISCUSSION QUESTIONS

CONSIDER THE SCRIPTURES READ, THEN ANSWER THE FOLLOWING QUESTIONS.

Why has Jesus's statement "one taken, one left" been so widely misunderstood? How does the comparison to Noah's day reshape our understanding of who is "taken"?

1

Why does Jesus emphasize ordinary daily activity at the moment of separation? What danger does normalcy present?

2

How can proximity to faith communities create a false sense of security?

3

What does watchfulness look like in everyday life, without fear or obsession?

4

NEXT

Prayer

Dear Father,
You warned us that separation would come
suddenly. Search our hearts.
Expose every place where familiarity has replaced
obedience
and routine has dulled readiness.
Teach us to live watchful lives marked by
obedience, repentance, and trust in You. When the
moment of separation comes, let us be found
ready. Prepare us now, so that when You reveal
what is true, we may be found ready.
We choose obedience over assumption,
faithfulness over familiarity,
and surrender over association.
In the Holy name of Jesus we pray,
Amen.

CHAPTER 16
THE COMING OF THE SON OF MAN ON THE CLOUDS

NEXT

"Then will appear the sign of the Son of Man in heaven. And then all the peoples of the earth will mourn when they see the Son of Man coming on the clouds of heaven, with power and great glory."

—Matthew 24:30 NIV

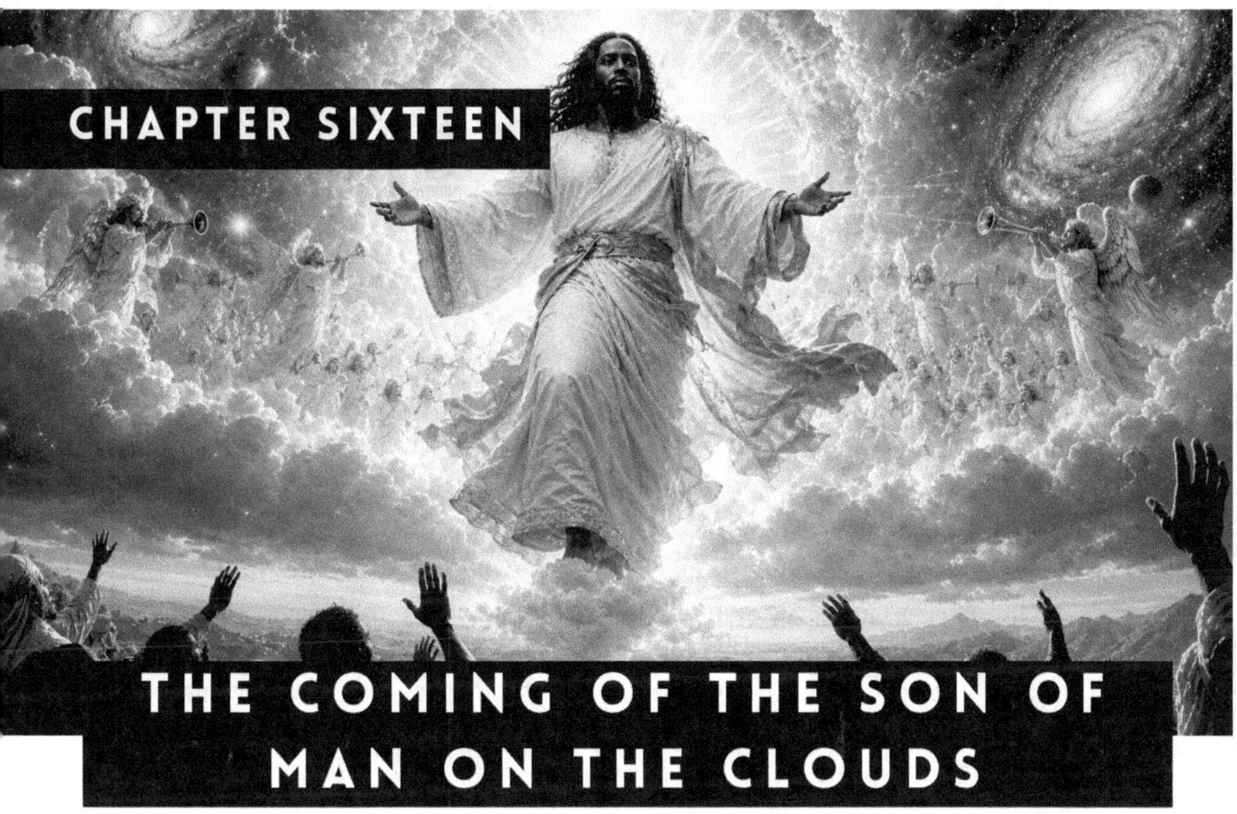

THE COMING OF THE SON OF MAN ON THE CLOUDS

Jesus does not describe His return as subtle, quiet, or hidden. There is no secrecy here, no private revelation, and no selective audience granted early access. Everyone will see Him. The same Jesus who was mocked, rejected, beaten, and crucified does not return as a suffering servant, but as a conquering King. This is the moment history has been leaning toward—the hinge upon which every age turns. Time does not merely continue; it yields.

The clouds matter because they have always mattered. Throughout the Bible, clouds signal God's presence, authority, and glory. God descended on Sinai within a heavy cloud. His glory filled the tabernacle in a cloud. Jesus ascended into heaven carried by a cloud. And at His ascension, angels declared with unmistakable clarity, *"This same Jesus... will come back in the same way you have seen Him go into heaven." [Acts 1:11 NIV]* The clouds announce continuity. The One who left is the One who returns. There is no replacement, no evolution, and no reinterpretation—only fulfillment.

Jesus tells us that before He is seen, the sign of the Son of Man appears in heaven. He does not define the sign because it will not require interpretation. It will not persuade skeptics or invite debate. It will declare. Heaven will signal what

NEXT

THE COMING OF THE SON OF MAN ON THE CLOUDS

"Then will appear the sign of the Son of Man in heaven. And then all the peoples of the earth will mourn when they see the Son of Man coming on the clouds of heaven, with power and great glory." —Matthew 24:30 NIV

earth cannot prevent. God will announce what humanity cannot silence. This sign does not ask for belief; it commands recognition.

When Jesus appears, He comes with power and great glory. This is not political power negotiated through systems, nor military might enforced by weapons. This is sovereign authority revealed. It is power that cannot be challenged and glory that cannot be diminished. Every throne, every ruler, every empire, and every system that once seemed immovable is suddenly exposed as small, temporary, and accountable.

Jesus tells us something sobering about the response of the world: *"All the tribes of the earth will mourn."* [Matt. 24:30 ESV] This mourning is not universal repentance. It is realization. The return of Christ exposes rejected truth, ignored warnings, and misplaced allegiance. For many, recognition arrives too late. What was dismissed as myth now stands visible in glory. Mourning follows because denial is no longer possible.

For the faithful, however, this moment is not terror. It is vindication. Jesus told His disciples, *"When these things begin to take place, stand up and lift up your heads."* [Luke 21:28 NIV] What terrifies the rebellious steadies the obedient. The King they trusted without seeing is now revealed. Faith becomes sight. Endurance meets reward.

This event is not metaphor, myth, or spiritualized abstraction. Jesus describes an event, and the apostles affirm it without hesitation. Paul writes that *"the Lord Jesus is revealed from heaven in blazing fire with His powerful angels."* [2 Thess. 1:7 NIV] Revelation echoes with finality, *"Look, He is coming with the clouds, and every eye will see Him."* [Rev. 1:7 NIV] This is not symbolic triumph. It is historical intervention.

Jesus never instructed believers to calculate the moment of His appearing. He instructed us to recognize the King. Readiness is not about charts or timelines; it is about allegiance. Those who belong to Him know Him when He appears.

146

THE COMING OF THE SON OF MAN ON THE CLOUDS

Recognition is relational, not analytical.

When Christ appears, ambiguity dies, debate ends and lies collapse. Truth stands visible and unchallenged. No one will ask if it is real and no one will wonder which side to choose. That question has already been answered by how one lived before this moment arrived.

The return of Jesus Christ is not only the end of suffering; it is the public validation of faithfulness. Everything endured in secret is acknowledged in glory. Every act of obedience unseen by the world is seen by the King. History does not close in silence. It concludes with revelation—Jesus Christ, coming on the clouds, with power and great glory.

"So Christ was sacrificed once to take away the sins of many; and he will appear a second time, not to bear sin, but to bring salvation to those who are waiting for him."
~ Hebrews 9:28 NIV

NEXT

KEY SCRIPTURES

Please read the scriptures, then answer the questions that follow.

ONE

MATTHEW 24:30–31 NIV

"Then will appear the sign of the Son of Man in heaven. And then all the peoples of the earth will mourn when they see the Son of Man coming on the clouds of heaven, with power and great glory. And he will send his angels with a loud trumpet call, and they will gather his elect from the four winds, from one end of the heavens to the other."

TWO

EXODUS 19:16–18 NIV

"On the morning of the third day there was thunder and lightning, with a thick cloud over the mountain, and a very loud trumpet blast. Everyone in the camp trembled. Then Moses led the people out of the camp to meet with God, and they stood at the foot of the mountain. Mount Sinai was covered with smoke, because the Lord descended on it in fire. The smoke billowed up from it like smoke from a furnace, and the whole mountain trembled violently."

THREE

DANIEL 7:13–14 NIV

"In my vision at night I looked, and there before me was one like a son of man, coming with the clouds of heaven. He approached the Ancient of Days and was led into his presence. He was given authority, glory and sovereign power; all nations and peoples of every language worshiped him. His dominion is an everlasting dominion that will not pass away, and his kingdom is one that will never be destroyed."

FOUR

LUKE 21:27–28 NIV

"At that time they will see the Son of Man coming in a cloud with power and great glory. When these things begin to take place, stand up and lift up your heads, because your redemption is drawing near."

FIVE

ACTS 1:9–11 NIV

"After he said this, he was taken up before their very eyes, and a cloud hid him from their sight. They were looking intently up into the sky as he was going, when suddenly two men dressed in white stood beside them. 'Men of Galilee,' they said, 'why do you stand here looking into the sky? This same Jesus, who has been taken from you into heaven, will come back in the same way you have seen him go into heaven.'"

NEXT

KEY SCRIPTURES

Please read the scriptures, then answer the questions that follow.

ONE

1 THESSALONIANS 4:16 NIV

"For the Lord himself will come down from heaven, with a loud command, with the voice of the archangel and with the trumpet call of God, and the dead in Christ will rise first."

TWO

2 THESSALONIANS 1:7–10 NIV

"This will happen when the Lord Jesus is revealed from heaven in blazing fire with his powerful angels. He will punish those who do not know God and do not obey the gospel of our Lord Jesus. They will be punished with everlasting destruction and shut out from the presence of the Lord and from the glory of his might on the day he comes to be glorified in his holy people and to be marveled at among all those who have believed. This includes you, because you believed our testimony to you."

THREE

PHILIPPIANS 2:9–11 NIV

"Therefore God exalted him to the highest place and gave him the name that is above every name, that at the name of Jesus every knee should bow, in heaven and on earth and under the earth, and every tongue acknowledge that Jesus Christ is Lord, to the glory of God the Father."

FOUR

HEBREWS 9:28 NIV

"So Christ was sacrificed once to take away the sins of many; and he will appear a second time, not to bear sin, but to bring salvation to those who are waiting for him."

FIVE

REVELATION 1:7 NIV

"'Look, he is coming with the clouds,' and 'every eye will see him, even those who pierced him'; and all peoples on earth 'will mourn because of him.' So shall it be! Amen."

GROUP DISCUSSION QUESTIONS

CONSIDER THE SCRIPTURES READ, THEN ANSWER THE FOLLOWING QUESTIONS.

ASK YOURSELF...

WRITE YOUR ANSWERS HERE....

Why is it important that Jesus's return is described as visible and public rather than secret? What false expectations does this correct?

Why do the nations mourn rather than celebrate at Christ's appearing?

How does the promise of public vindication strengthen endurance now?

What does it mean to be "ready" for Christ's return apart from knowing dates or timelines?

How do the clouds connect Jesus's return to God's authority throughout Scripture?

NEXT

Prayer

Lord Jesus,

We confess that we believe You will come in glory,
with power that silences every lie and authority
that ends every debate.
Prepare our hearts now to recognize You then.
Strip away every compromise that would not stand
in Your presence. Strengthen our endurance so
that when You appear, we lift our heads with
confidence, not regret.
When faith is tested and obedience is costly,
ground us in the promise of Your appearing. May
what the world mourns be the joy of our hearts—
the vindication of faith, the fulfillment of hope,
and the revelation of our King.
We wait with trust, we endure with confidence, and
we lift our heads in hope.
Come, Lord Jesus.
Amen.

CHAPTER 17 ARMAGEDDON --WAR, SYMBOL, OR FINAL JUDGMENT?

NEXT

"Then they gathered the kings together to the place that in Hebrew is called Armageddon."

—REVELATION 16:16

ARMAGEDDON--WAR, SYMBOL, OR FINAL JUDGMENT?

Few words in Scripture carry the cultural weight of Armageddon. It has been imagined as a nuclear battlefield, a political showdown, a global military conflict, or a cinematic apocalypse where the fate of the world hangs in suspense. Yet Scripture itself treats Armageddon with remarkable restraint. It is mentioned only once by name, and when it appears, it is not dramatized. It is precise, deliberate, and sober. The power of Armageddon is not in spectacle, but in what it reveals.

Armageddon is not described as a prolonged war between equal forces. It is not a contest to determine who might prevail. It is not chaos spiraling beyond God's control. Revelation does not dwell on strategies, troop movements, casualties, or tactics. Instead, it emphasizes a single action: a gathering. The focus is not on battle mechanics, but on the consolidation of rebellion.

Revelation 16:16 tells us that the kings of the earth are gathered together. This gathering is not accidental. Throughout Scripture, God allows opposition to assemble openly so that it may be judged decisively.   Rebellion concentrates

NEXT

ARMAGEDDON--WAR, SYMBOL, OR FINAL JUDGMENT?

"Then they gathered the kings together to the place that in Hebrew is called Armageddon."
—Revelation 16:16 NIV

before it collapses. Psalm 2 foreshadows this moment when it declares, *"The kings of the earth rise up… against the Lord and against His Anointed."* Armageddon is the culmination of humanity's resistance to God's authority—the final alignment of power against God.

Deception plays a critical role in this moment. Revelation makes clear that demonic spirits go out to the kings of the whole world to gather them for battle. [Rev. 16:14] Armageddon is not merely military; it is deeply spiritual. The nations are deceived into believing resistance is still possible, even after Christ has been revealed in glory. Deception does not end with the return of Christ—it intensifies just before it collapses completely.

Scripture allows us to understand Armageddon as both geographically real and theologically profound. Har-Megiddo (Encyclopedia, 2026) refers to a real location, historically associated with decisive battles and it lies approximately eighteen miles southeast of Haifa in northern Israel.

Yet Revelation presses beyond geography into meaning. Armageddon represents the convergence of global power, the exposure of hardened rebellion, and the inevitability of judgment. Whether armies gather physically, ideologically, or systemically, the outcome does not change.

When Revelation finally describes the so-called battle, it is strikingly brief. In Revelation 19, the beast is captured and thrown alive into the lake of fire. There is no prolonged conflict. No suspense. No exchange of blows. Christ does not struggle. His authority alone ends the rebellion. The "battle" is not about force—it is about revelation. The presence of the King is enough.

Scripture still calls this moment war because it represents the final refusal to submit. Armageddon is humanity's last attempt to assert autonomy from God. It is the ultimate declaration of independence spoken against God's authority. And it fails instantly. Rebellion is not defeated by superior

155

ARMAGEDDON--WAR, SYMBOL, OR FINAL JUDGMENT?

weapons, but by the undeniable reality of Jesus Christ's reign.

Armageddon marks judgment without ambiguity. It is the end of false power, the removal of counterfeit authority, and the collapse of systems built on deception. This judgment does not bring indiscriminate destruction. It is targeted and just. God does not judge ignorance; He judges defiance. Those gathered are not confused seekers, but willful resisters of truth.

Even here, hope is not absent. God does not destroy the earth; He clears it. Judgment is not annihilation. It is preparation. Armageddon is not the end of creation—it is the clearing of the stage for the Kingdom to reign. What is removed is not humanity itself, but rebellion that refuses to yield.

Victory does not depend on human resistance, activism, or survival. It depends entirely on Jesus's authority. This moment reminds believers that evil may be loud, but it is temporary; that power gathered against God is already defeated; and that Christ reigns without rival.

Armageddon asks one final question of humanity, and it allows no middle ground: will you submit, or will you resist until the end? At that point, neutrality no longer exists.

"And then the lawless one will be revealed, whom the Lord Jesus will overthrow with the breath of his mouth and destroy by the splendor of his coming."
~ 2 Thessalonians 2:8 NIV

NEXT

KEY SCRIPTURES

Please read the scriptures, then answer the questions that follow.

ONE

REVELATION 16:16 NIV

"Then they gathered the kings together to the place that in Hebrew is called Armageddon."

TWO

REVELATION 19:19–20 NIV

"Then I saw the beast and the kings of the earth and their armies gathered together to wage war against the rider on the horse and his army. But the beast was captured, and with it the false prophet who had performed the signs on its behalf. With these signs he had deluded those who had received the mark of the beast and worshiped its image. The two of them were thrown alive into the fiery lake of burning sulfur."

THREE

PSALM 2:1–6 NIV

"Why do the nations conspire, and the peoples plot in vain? The kings of the earth rise up and the rulers band together against the Lord and against his anointed, saying, 'Let us break their chains and throw off their shackles.' The One enthroned in heaven laughs; the Lord scoffs at them. He rebukes them in his anger and terrifies them in his wrath, saying, 'I have installed my king on Zion, my holy mountain.'"

FOUR

JOEL 3:9,14–16 NIV

"Proclaim this among the nations: Prepare for war! Rouse the warriors! Let all the fighting men draw near and attack. Multitudes, multitudes in the valley of decision! For the day of the Lord is near in the valley of decision. The sun and moon will be darkened, and the stars no longer shine. The Lord will roar from Zion and thunder from Jerusalem; the earth and the heavens will tremble. But the Lord will be a refuge for his people, a stronghold for the people of Israel."

FIVE

ZECHARIAH 14:2–4 NIV

"I will gather all the nations to Jerusalem to fight against it; the city will be captured, the houses ransacked, and the women raped. Half of the city will go into exile, but the rest of the people will not be taken from the city. Then the Lord will go out and fight against those nations, as he fights on a day of battle. On that day his feet will stand on the Mount of Olives, east of Jerusalem, and the Mount of Olives will be split in two from east to west, forming a great valley, with half of the mountain moving north and half moving south."

NEXT

KEY SCRIPTURES

Please read the scriptures, then answer the questions that follow.

ONE

2 THESSALONIANS 2:8 NIV

"And then the lawless one will be revealed, whom the Lord Jesus will overthrow with the breath of his mouth and destroy by the splendor of his coming."

TWO

REVELATION 14:19–20 NIV

"The angel swung his sickle on the earth, gathered its grapes and threw them into the great winepress of God's wrath. They were trampled in the winepress outside the city, and blood flowed out of the press, rising as high as the horses' bridles for a distance of 1,600 stadia."

THREE

ISAIAH 2:19–21 NIV

"People will flee to caves in the rocks and to holes in the ground from the fearful presence of the Lord and the splendor of his majesty, when he rises to shake the earth. In that day people will throw away to the moles and bats their idols of silver and idols of gold, which they made to worship. They will flee to caverns in the rocks and to the overhanging crags from the fearful presence of the Lord and the splendor of his majesty, when he rises to shake the earth."

FOUR

ISAIAH 66:15–16 NIV

"See, the Lord is coming with fire, and his chariots are like a whirlwind; he will bring down his anger with fury, and his rebuke with flames of fire. For with fire and with his sword the Lord will execute judgment on all people, and many will be those slain by the Lord."

FIVE

DANIEL 2:44–45 NIV

"In the time of those kings, the God of heaven will set up a kingdom that will never be destroyed, nor will it be left to another people. It will crush all those kingdoms and bring them to an end, but it will itself endure forever. This is the meaning of the vision of the rock cut out of a mountain, but not by human hands—a rock that broke the iron, the bronze, the clay, the silver and the gold to pieces. 'The great God has shown the king what will take place in the future. The dream is true and its interpretation is trustworthy.'"

NEXT

GROUP DISCUSSION QUESTIONS

CONSIDER THE SCRIPTURES READ, THEN ANSWER THE FOLLOWING QUESTIONS.

Why does Scripture focus more on the gathering at Armageddon than on the battle itself?
What does that reveal about the nature of God's victory?

1

How does deception enable rebellion to persist even after Jesus returns in the most
spectacular display of power?

2

Why is Armageddon best understood as judgment rather than a conventional war?

3

What does it mean that Christ wins without fighting?

4

159

NEXT

Prayer

Sovereign Lord,
You reign without rival, and no power that gathers
against You can stand.
When rebellion gathers and deception
consolidates,
anchor our hearts in Your unchallenged reign.
Guard our hearts from fear and false urgency.
Give us discernment instead of panic, and
confidence instead of dread.
Teach us to remain faithful, knowing the outcome
is already decided.
As the world chooses resistance over submission,
we confess that we will stand firmly with You.
We declare that You are King and
Your Kingdom stands forever.
We choose allegiance—now and always.
In the name of Jesus Christ,
Amen.

CHAPTER 18 THE MILLENNIAL KINGDOM -- THE 1,000-YEAR REIGN

NEXT

"Then I saw thrones and seated
on them were those to whom
the authority to judge was
committed. Also I saw the souls
of those who had been beheaded
for the testimony of Jesus and
for the word of God, and those
who had not worshiped the
beast or its image and had not
received its mark on their
foreheads or their hands. They
came to life and reigned with
Christ for a thousand years. "

—Revelation 20:4 ESV

THE MILLENNIAL KINGDOM – THE 1,000-YEAR REIGN

The Millennial Kingdom is not an afterthought tucked at the edge of prophecy. It is the fulfillment of promises spoken across generations. The prophets saw it from afar and spoke of it with longing. The apostles anticipated it with expectation. Jesus Himself taught His disciples to pray toward it when He said, *"Your kingdom come. Your will be done, on earth as it is in heaven."* The Millennial Kingdom is the answer to that prayer. What was pleaded for in faith becomes visible in history.

Revelation speaks with deliberate clarity: Jesus reigns for a thousand years. This is the Kingdom that the Israelites longed for, and it is not symbolic abstraction. It is a real, historical, visible reign of Jesus Christ on the earth as the promised Messiah. He rules personally, not metaphorically. He governs justly, not partially, and reigns publicly, not invisibly. The Kingdom of God is no longer resisted, debated, or postponed. It was established at the Cross.

163

THE MILLENNIAL KINGDOM – THE 1,000-YEAR REIGN

"...They came to life and reigned with Christ for a thousand years."
—Revelation 20:4 ESV

Scripture makes a crucial distinction regarding Satan during this period. *"He seized the dragon… and bound him for a thousand years."* [Rev. 20:2 ESV] Satan is restrained, not destroyed. This matters deeply. The Millennial Kingdom exposes what the world looks like when deception is removed. Satan will no longer be the cause of every injustice. Righteous rule is tested in full light, without the constant fog of spiritual manipulation.

The prophets give us a glimpse of life under this reign. Isaiah declares that Christ will judge with righteousness and equity, and that creation itself will rest. The wolf dwells with the lamb, violence ceases, and oppression ends. [Isaiah 65:17-25] Justice is no longer theoretical or delayed—it is enacted. This is not symbolic justice preached from afar. It is truth enforced at the center of power. Jesus governs not by compromise, but by righteousness.

The reign of Christ is not solitary. Revelation tells us that the faithful reign with Him. *"They will be priests of God and of Christ and will reign with Him."* [Rev. 20:6 NIV] This authority is not celebrity power or dominance.

It is servant leadership refined through endurance. Those who suffered without abandoning faith now steward righteousness. What was forged in trial is entrusted with governance. Suffering is proven preparation.

The thousand-year duration is not an arbitrary number. Scripture does not speculate; it declares. The length reveals God's patience, order, and intentionality. The Millennial Kingdom allows history to witness what righteous leadership produces, what obedience restores, and what justice looks like when power is pure. It answers every accusation ever leveled against God's rule. The record is settled in the open.

During this reign, creation is renewed but not yet finalized. Lifespans increase, peace expands, and the earth heals. Yet sin is restrained, not erased. Death is delayed, not abolished. The Millennial Kingdom is a demonstration, not the finale. It

NEXT

THE MILLENNIAL KINGDOM – THE 1,000-YEAR REIGN

prepares the stage for the final restoration still to come.

The Millennial Kingdom matters profoundly. It affirms that God keeps His promises to Israel, restores the earth rather than abandoning it, and rules history rather than escaping it. Redemption does not mean removal. God redeems what He created. The Kingdom does not discard the world; it reclaims it.

At the close of the Millennial rule, Scripture records that Satan is released briefly. The reason is piercing in its clarity. Even in perfect conditions, rebellion remains a choice. Environment alone does not produce righteousness. Evil is not caused solely by suffering or injustice. It is rooted in the human heart. Every excuse collapses under the weight of truth.

For the faithful, the Millennial Reign of Jesus Christ stands as undeniable proof. Obedience is rewarded, endurance has purpose, and justice is not postponed forever. What was mocked is honored. What was hidden is revealed. Christ reigns —and His people reign with Him.

Humanity has long asked a single question: *"What would the world look like if God were truly in charge?"* The Millennial Kingdom answers without apology: **this.**

NEXT

KEY SCRIPTURES

Please read the scriptures, then answer the questions that follow.

ONE

REVELATION 20:4 NIV

"I saw thrones on which were seated those who had been given authority to judge. And I saw the souls of those who had been beheaded because of their testimony about Jesus and because of the word of God. They had not worshiped the beast or its image and had not received its mark on their foreheads or their hands. They came to life and reigned with Christ a thousand years."

TWO

ISAIAH 2:4 NIV

"He will judge between the nations and will settle disputes for many peoples. They will beat their swords into plowshares and their spears into pruning hooks. Nation will not take up sword against nation, nor will they train for war anymore."

THREE

ISAIAH 11:6–7 NIV

"The wolf will live with the lamb, the leopard will lie down with the goat, the calf and the lion and the yearling together; and a little child will lead them. The cow will feed with the bear, their young will lie down together, and the lion will eat straw like the ox."

FOUR

ISAIAH 9:7 NIV

"Of the greatness of his government and peace there will be no end. He will reign on David's throne and over his kingdom, establishing and upholding it with justice and righteousness from that time on and forever. The zeal of the Lord Almighty will accomplish this."

FIVE

DANIEL 7:13–14 NIV

"In my vision at night I looked, and there before me was one like a son of man, coming with the clouds of heaven. He approached the Ancient of Days and was led into his presence. He was given authority, glory and sovereign power; all nations and peoples of every language worshiped him. His dominion is an everlasting dominion that will not pass away, and his kingdom is one that will never be destroyed."

NEXT

KEY SCRIPTURES

Please read the scriptures, then answer the questions that follow.

ONE

DANIEL 7:27 NIV

"Then the sovereignty, power and greatness of all the kingdoms under heaven will be handed over to the holy people of the Most High. His kingdom will be an everlasting kingdom, and all rulers will worship and obey him.'"

TWO

MATTHEW 6:9–10 NIV

"This, then, is how you should pray: 'Our Father in heaven, hallowed be your name, your kingdom come, your will be done, on earth as it is in heaven.'"

THREE

ISAIAH 65:20 NIV

"Never again will there be in it an infant who lives but a few days, or an old man who does not live out his years; the one who dies at a hundred will be thought a mere child; the one who fails to reach a hundred will be considered accursed."

FOUR

1 CORINTHIANS 15:24–26 NIV

"Then the end will come, when he hands over the kingdom to God the Father after he has destroyed all dominion, authority and power. For he must reign until he has put all his enemies under his feet. The last enemy to be destroyed is death."

FIVE

REVELATION 5:9–10 NIV

"And they sang a new song, saying: 'You are worthy to take the scroll and to open its seals, because you were slain, and with your blood you purchased for God persons from every tribe and language and people and nation. You have made them to be a kingdom and priests to serve our God, and they will reign on the earth.'"

NEXT

GROUP DISCUSSION QUESTIONS

CONSIDER THE SCRIPTURES READ, THEN ANSWER THE FOLLOWING QUESTIONS.

ONE

Why does Scripture emphasize a literal, earthly reign of Jesus rather than immediate eternal finality? What does this reveal about God's purposes for history?

TWO

What does Satan's binding—and later release—teach us about the nature of God?

THREE

Why are those who endured suffering entrusted with authority in the Kingdom?

FOUR

How does the Millennial Kingdom answer humanity's question about God's rule?

FIVE

Why is the Millennial Kingdom necessary before the final new heaven and new earth?

SIX

How does reigning with Christ reshape our understanding of suffering and faithfulness now?

SEVEN

How does Christ's coming Kingdom shape our sense of justice now?

NEXT

Prayer

Righteous King,
Thank You that Your reign will be righteous, visible,
and unopposed. Thank You that obedience is not
forgotten, endurance is not wasted,
and that justice is not postponed forever.
Prepare us now for what You will entrust later.
Refine our hearts so we may steward rightly. Teach
us to submit joyfully to Your rule today
so we may reign faithfully with You tomorrow. We
align our lives with Your rule now, so that we may
reign with You then.
Your Kingdom come—Your will be done.
On earth, as it is in heaven.
You reign.
And we rejoice.
In Your sovereign name—Jesus,
Amen.

CHAPTER 19 THE FINAL REBELLION AND SATAN'S DEFEAT

NEXT

"When the thousand years are over, Satan will be released from his prison and will go out to deceive the nations in the four corners of the earth—Gog and Magog—and to gather them for battle. In number they are like the sand on the seashore. They marched across the breadth of the earth and surrounded the camp of God's people, the city he loves. But fire came down from heaven and devoured them. And the devil, who deceived them, was thrown into the lake of burning sulfur, where the beast and the false prophet had been thrown. They will be tormented day and night for ever and ever."

—Revelation 20:7–10

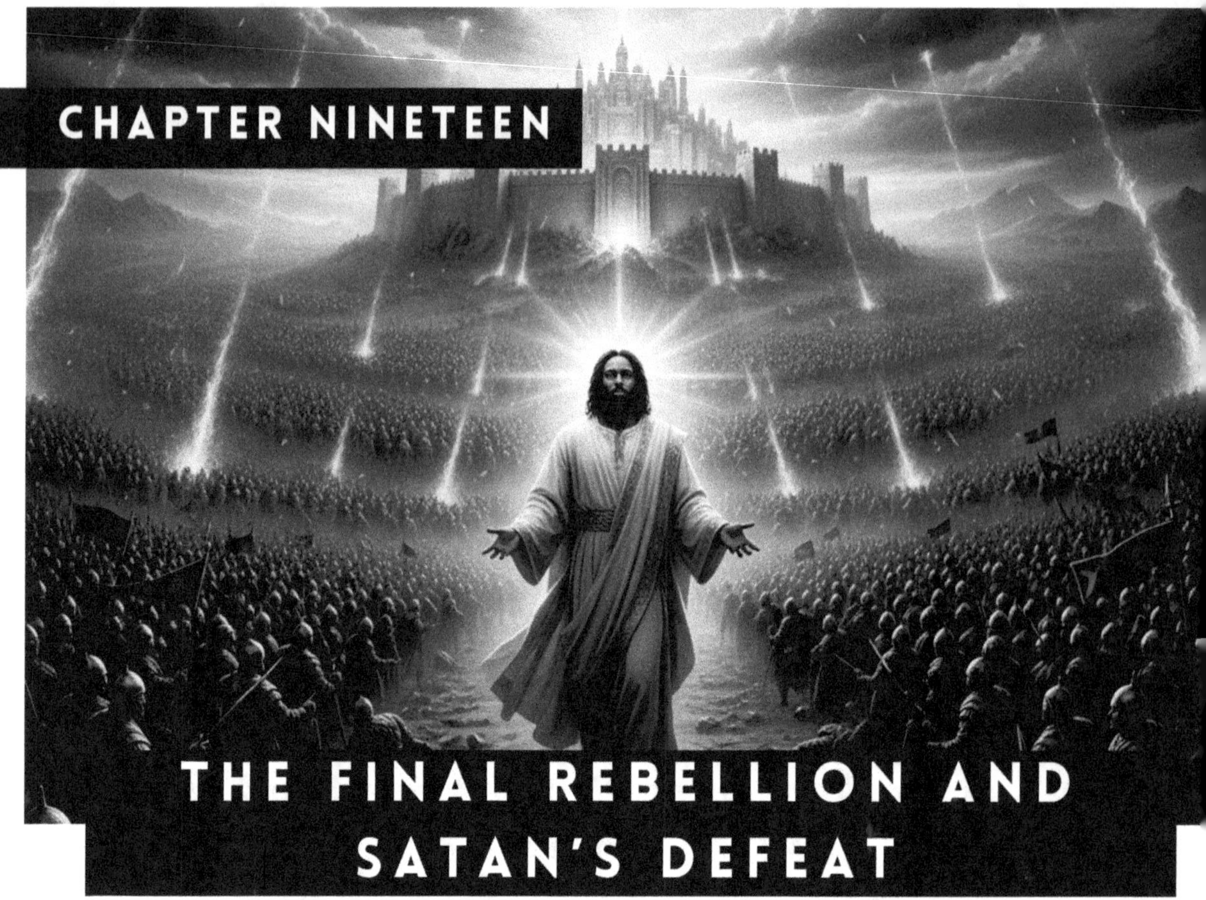

THE FINAL REBELLION AND SATAN'S DEFEAT

After a thousand years of righteous rule, Scripture delivers one of its most sobering revelations. Satan is released for a short time. This release is not a failure in God's plan, or a lapse in His control. It is intentional, measured, and revealing. The Millennial Kingdom has already answered every accusation against God's justice. Now one final question must be settled: Is *rebellion in Man caused by Satan, or by the heart?*

Revelation tells us that Satan goes out once more to deceive the nations—to gather those who still choose resistance after living under perfect governance, abundant peace, and visible righteousness. This is the final exposure. Even with deception restrained for a thousand years, Christ reigning openly, and with justice enforced without corruption, some hearts remain unwilling to submit. This rebellion is not born out of suffering. It is born from refusal.

The nations gather again—not because they were oppressed, but because they desire autonomy. Scripture calls this assembly Gog and Magog, a symbolic name for the totality of rebellion across history. It is not about geography or a cruel

NEXT

THE FINAL REBELLION AND SATAN'S DEFEAT

ruler. It is about human posturing against God's Authority. It is the final "No" spoken to God and it ends instantly.

There is no drawn-out war, dramatic exchange, or suspense. Fire comes down from heaven and consumes those who chose rebellion over submission to a just and righteous King. Satan, the deceiver of the nations, is finally and permanently removed—thrown into the lake of fire where the beast and the false prophet already are. He is not just restrained anymore but is eradicated. Deception's reign is over and the voice of evil is silenced. The enemy who accused, distorted, and resisted from Eden onward is defeated without appeal.

This moment proves forever that rebellion is not situational but intentional. God's justice stands vindicated before all creation and every excuse collapses under the weight of it.

"And the devil, who deceived them, was thrown into the lake of burning sulfur, where the beast and the false prophet had been thrown. They will be tormented day and night for ever and ever."
~ Revelation 20:10 NIV

KEY SCRIPTURES

Please read the scriptures, then answer the questions that follow.

ONE

REVELATION 20:1–3 NIV

"And I saw an angel coming down out of heaven, having the key to the Abyss and holding in his hand a great chain. He seized the dragon, that ancient serpent, who is the devil, or Satan, and bound him for a thousand years. He threw him into the Abyss, and locked and sealed it over him, to keep him from deceiving the nations anymore until the thousand years were ended. After that, he must be set free for a short time."

TWO

PSALM 2:1-6 NIV

"Why do the nations conspire and the peoples plot in vain? The kings of the earth rise up and the rulers band together against the Lord and against his anointed, saying, 'Let us break their chains and throw off their shackles.' The One enthroned in heaven laughs; the Lord scoffs at them. He rebukes them in his anger and terrifies them in his wrath, saying, 'I have installed my king on Zion, my holy mountain.'"

THREE

EZEKIEL 38:18-23 NIV

"This is what will happen in that day: When Gog attacks the land of Israel, my hot anger will be aroused, declares the Sovereign Lord. In my zeal and fiery wrath I declare that at that time there shall be a great earthquake in the land of Israel. The fish in the sea, the birds in the sky, the beasts of the field, every creature that moves along the ground, and all the people on the face of the earth will tremble at my presence. The mountains will be overturned, the cliffs will crumble and every wall will fall to the ground. I will summon a sword against Gog on all my mountains, declares the Sovereign Lord. Every man's sword will be against his brother. I will execute judgment on him with plague and bloodshed; I will pour down torrents of rain, hailstones and burning sulfur on him and on his troops and on the many nations with him. And so I will show my greatness and my holiness, and I will make myself known in the sight of many nations. Then they will know that I am the Lord.'"

NEXT

GROUP DISCUSSION QUESTIONS

CONSIDER THE SCRIPTURES READ, THEN ANSWER THE FOLLOWING QUESTIONS.

Why is Satan released after the Millennial period instead of being destroyed immediately?

1

What does the final rebellion reveal about the nature of sin and human choice?

2

How does the instant defeat of rebellion reshape common ideas about spiritual warfare?

3

Why is it important that deception is fully removed before final judgment?

4

175

NEXT

Prayer

Father God,
You have shown us that rebellion is not born from
suffering alone,
but from hearts that refuse to submit even in the
light of truth.
Search us and expose every quiet resistance, every
hidden excuse, and every delayed obedience.
Teach us to yield now—freely, humbly, and fully.
We thank You that deception will not reign forever
and that evil will not have the final word.
Strengthen our allegiance so that we stand with
Jesus
not because resistance has ended, but because
love has chosen submission.
We bow now, so we will not resist then.
In the name of Jesus Christ,
Amen.

CHAPTER 20
THE GREAT WHITE THRONE JUDGMENT

"Then I saw a great white throne and Him who was seated on it. The earth and the heavens fled from His presence, and there was no place for them."

—Revelation 20:11 NIV

CHAPTER TWENTY

THE GREAT WHITE THRONE JUDGMENT

After rebellion is gathered and crushed, after false power collapses and deception is silenced, Scripture does not fade into ambiguity. It moves with terrifying clarity into the final scene of accountability. John sees *a great white throne*—not hidden, not symbolic, and not negotiable. It is white, because it's pure. It is great, because its authority is absolute. This is not a throne of war. It is a throne of judgment and before it, nothing remains unaccountable.

The One seated on the throne is not named because no name is required. Authority radiates from His presence alone. Earth and heaven flee, not because they are destroyed, but because they can no longer conceal anything. Every refuge collapses and every hiding place dissolves. There is nowhere left to stand except before truth itself. Creation yields to the Creator, and time gives way to eternity.

This judgment is final because it is comprehensive. John writes that the dead, great and small, stand before the throne. Status no longer matters. Influence evaporates.

THE GREAT WHITE THRONE JUDGMENT

"Then I saw a great white throne and Him who was seated on it. The earth and the heavens fled from His presence, and there was no place for them."
—Revelation 20:11 NIV

Power offers no protection. Wealth carries no weight. The categories that once defined humanity dissolve into a single reality: every person stands alone before God. It is the moment of the great equalizer where truth is enforced.

"And I saw the dead, great and small, standing before the throne, and books were opened. Another book was opened, which is the book of life. The dead were judged according to what they had done as recorded in the books." [Rev. 20:12 NIV] Lives are not judged by vague impressions or emotional memory, but by what was done—by choices made in light of truth received. And then another book is opened: the Book of Life. This is the dividing line. This judgment is not arbitrary or impulsive. It is precise. Those whose names are written in the Book of Life belong to Christ. Those whose names are absent face judgment not for ignorance, but for refusal.

This moment exposes a critical truth: Salvation has always been relational, not transactional. No one stands condemned for lack of information. They stand condemned for rejecting the truth they were given. The Great White Throne does not judge sin alone—it judges defiance. Grace and mercy were offered and witness was given. Now response is accounted for.

Death itself is summoned and judged. The grave releases its claim. The final enemy is stripped of authority and cast into the lake of fire. Death will no longer reign. It is judged and removed. What once ruled humanity is itself ruled by Jesus Christ. Nothing remains unresolved.

The lake of fire is the final scene. Scripture calls it the second death because there is no appeal beyond it. This is not annihilation, but separation —eternal exclusion from the presence of God. The seriousness of this moment cannot be softened without betraying Scripture. Love does not negate justice, and mercy does not erase accountability. The cross does not abolish judgment; it defines the

THE GREAT WHITE THRONE JUDGMENT

only escape from it.

And yet, even here, the righteousness of God is undeniable. No one is treated unjustly. No one is condemned unfairly. Every judgment rendered aligns perfectly with truth. God does not condemn the unwillingly deceived. He judges the persistently defiant. What is destroyed is not humanity itself, but rebellion that refuses reconciliation.

For the faithful, the Great White Throne is not terrifying. Judgment has already been faced at the cross. Condemnation has already been carried by Christ. This throne does not threaten those who belong to Him; it vindicates them. Justice is finally seen to be complete. Evil is finally judged and suffering is finally explained—not always by reason, but by resolution.

The Great White Throne marks the irreversible end of rebellion and the irreversible beginning of restoration. What follows is renewal, inheritance, and a dwelling place. God does not end history with destruction, but with order restored and truth enthroned.

This scene asks one final, unavoidable question of every soul: Where is your name written? It doesn't ask what you believed in theory or what you claimed in public, but where your allegiance truly lie. Because when the Great White Throne appears, delay is over, neutrality is gone, and eternity begins—not as speculation, but as reality.

> "But I tell you that everyone will have to give account on the day of judgment for every empty word they have spoken."
> ~ Matthew 12:36 NIV

NEXT

KEY SCRIPTURES

Please read the scriptures, then answer the questions that follow.

ONE

REVELATION 20:11-13 NIV (ALSO VERSES 14-15)

"Then I saw a great white throne and him who was seated on it. The earth and the heavens fled from his presence, and there was no place for them. And I saw the dead, great and small, standing before the throne, and books were opened. Another book was opened, which is the book of life. The dead were judged according to what they had done as recorded in the books."

TWO

DANIEL 7:9-10 NIV

"As I looked, 'thrones were set in place, and the Ancient of Days took his seat. His clothing was as white as snow; the hair of his head was white like wool. His throne was flaming with fire, and its wheels were all ablaze. A river of fire was flowing, coming out from before him. Thousands upon thousands attended him; ten thousand times ten thousand stood before him. The court was seated, and the books were opened.'"

THREE

MATTHEW 25:31-33 NIV (ALSO VERSES 34-46)

"When the Son of Man comes in his glory, and all the angels with him, he will sit on his glorious throne. All the nations will be gathered before him, and he will separate the people one from another as a shepherd separates the sheep from the goats. He will put the sheep on his right and the goats on his left."

FOUR

MATTHEW 12:36-37 NIV

"But I tell you that everyone will have to give account on the day of judgment for every empty word they have spoken. For by your words you will be acquitted, and by your words you will be condemned."

FIVE

ROMANS 2:5-11 NIV

"But because of your stubbornness and your unrepentant heart, you are storing up wrath against yourself for the day of God's wrath, when his righteous judgment will be revealed. God 'will repay each person according to what they have done.' To those who by persistence in doing good seek glory, honor and immortality, he will give eternal life. But for those who are self-seeking and who reject the truth and follow evil, there will be wrath and anger. There will be trouble and distress for every human being who does evil: first for the Jew, then for the Gentile; but glory, honor and peace for everyone who does good: first for the Jew, then for the Gentile. For God does not show favoritism."

NEXT

KEY SCRIPTURES

Please read the scriptures, then answer the questions that follow.

ONE

2 CORINTHIANS 5:10 NIV

"For we must all appear before the judgment seat of Christ, so that each of us may receive what is due us for the things done while in the body, whether good or bad."

TWO

DANIEL 12:2 NIV

"Multitudes who sleep in the dust of the earth will awake: some to everlasting life, others to shame and everlasting contempt."

THREE

JOHN 5:28-29 NIV

"Do not be amazed at this, for a time is coming when all who are in their graves will hear his voice and come out—those who have done what is good will rise to live, and those who have done what is evil will rise to be condemned."

FOUR

ROMANS 14:10-12 NIV

"You, then, why do you judge your brother or sister? Or why do you treat them with contempt? For we will all stand before God's judgment seat. It is written: 'As surely as I live,' says the Lord, 'every knee will bow before me; every tongue will acknowledge God.' So then, each of us will give an account of ourselves to God."

FIVE

JOHN 5:22-27 NIV

"Moreover, the Father judges no one, but has entrusted all judgment to the Son, that all may honor the Son just as they honor the Father. Whoever does not honor the Son does not honor the Father, who sent him. Very truly I tell you, whoever hears my word and believes him who sent me has eternal life and will not be judged but has crossed over from death to life. Very truly I tell you, a time is coming and has now come when the dead will hear the voice of the Son of God and those who hear will live. For as the Father has life in himself, so he has granted the Son also to have life in himself. And he has given him authority to judge because he is the Son of Man."

NEXT

GROUP DISCUSSION QUESTIONS

CONSIDER THE SCRIPTURES READ, THEN ANSWER THE FOLLOWING QUESTIONS.

Why does Scripture emphasize the opening of books at the final judgment?

1

How does the Book of Life clarify the nature of salvation and accountability?

2

Why is it important that death itself is judged and removed?

3

How does the Great White Throne change how we view justice, mercy, and eternity?

4

184

NEXT

Prayer

Righteous Judge and Merciful Savior,
You see all things and forget nothing. Before
Your throne, truth stands clear and justice is
complete.
We thank You that our judgment has been borne
by Christ.
Keep our hearts humble, our lives faithful, and
our message honest.
Strengthen us to stand firm, to speak truth while
time remains,
and to rest in Your righteousness when all
accounts are settled.
Thank You that our names are written in the
Book of Life,
and our lives reflect allegiance to You alone.
In the name of Jesus Christ,
Amen.

CHAPTER 21
A NEW HEAVEN AND A NEW EARTH

NEXT

"Then I saw 'a new heaven and a new earth,' for the first heaven and the first earth had passed away, and there was no longer any sea."
—Revelation 21:1 NIV

A NEW HEAVEN AND A NEW EARTH

The final act of God is not the abandonment of creation, but its restoration. Scripture does not conclude with escape but with renewal. What sin fractured is healed. What corruption touched is made whole. What was lost is returned—this time without the possibility of loss again. This is the completion of redemption. History does not dissolve into nothingness; it is gathered, purified, and fulfilled.

When John says the heaven and earth are made new, he does not mean unfamiliar or unrecognizable. He means new—not transformed or morphed from the original. Just as resurrection restores the body without erasing identity, the new heaven and new earth restore creation without discarding its essence. God does not look at what He made and call it a failure. He calls it finished—properly, finally, and forever.

John tells us that the former heaven and earth pass away, and this is significant. Paul explains *"For the creation was subjected to frustration, not by its own choice, but by the will of the one who subjected it, in hope that the creation itself will be liberated from its bondage to decay and brought into the freedom and glory of the children of God." [Romans 8:20-21 NIV]*

188

A NEW HEAVEN AND A NEW EARTH

"Then I saw a new heaven and a new earth, for the first heaven and the first earth had passed away, and there was no longer any sea."
—Revelation 21:1

Decay ends and death loses its claim on us. The groaning that has echoed through the universe since the fall is finally silenced. Creation exhales as it is decisively released from the curse of death.

Then John notes something startling: there is no longer any sea. [Rev. 21:1 NIV] In Scripture, the sea is not merely water. It represents chaos, unrest, separation, and threat. The sea has swallowed ships, separated people, and has demonstrated unrestrained control through extreme weather conditions. Its absence is not merely geographical—it is intentionally seen and inserted for our understanding. Chaos will no longer threaten, separation will be nonexistent, and uncertainty will vanish. Peace will be our permanent home.

At the center of this new creation stands the fulfillment of humanity's deepest longing: God dwells with His people. *"Now the dwelling of God is with humanity."* [Rev. 21:3 CSB] There will be no need for a temple to contain this, and no mediator will stand between us and God. John says it this way: "And I heard a loud voice from the throne saying, *"Look! God's dwelling place is now among the people, and he will dwell with them. They will be his people, and God himself will be with them and be their God."* [Rev. 21:3 NIV] God does not visit—He dwells with us. What was lost in Eden is restored in fullness. Our communion will never end and God's presence with us will not be interrupted.

God, Himself, declares the end of all that has broken us. There will be no more death, no more mourning, no more crying, and no more pain. These are not minor details. They are real wounds—now permanently undone. Death, grief, trauma, and fear are all gone—never to return. The enemies that haunted every generation are dismissed forever.

This new creation also carries moral clarity. Within its walls, corruption is absent, deception is silenced, and destruction is rendered powerless. This exclusion is for the protection of

A NEW HEAVEN AND A NEW EARTH

its inhabitants and is born of holiness. This place is not fragile. It does not need constant defense against corruption. It stands secure in righteousness.

Those who feared losing themselves or their lives misunderstood eternity. God's Word presents continuity, not cancellation. We are known, named, and recognized. Resurrection restores identity without weakness, personality without sin, and uniqueness without fracture. We are fully ourselves—finally free.

Then Jesus speaks words that echo louder than creation itself: *"It is done. I am the Alpha and the Omega, the Beginning and the End. To the thirsty I will give water without cost from the spring of the water of life. Those who are victorious will inherit all this, and I will be their God, and they will be my children. But the cowardly, the unbelieving, the vile, the murderers, the sexually immoral, those who practice magic arts, the idolaters and all liars—they will be consigned to the fiery lake of burning sulfur. This is the second death."* [Rev. 21:6-8 NIV] It is a final decree. Done. History reaches its true conclusion. Every promise will be fulfilled, every tear dried, and every injustice resolved. God's work is complete.

This vision matters now because eternity reshapes how we live in time. Those of us who believe in restoration endure suffering without despair. We pursue justice without cynicism. We love without fear of loss. And we invest in what lasts. Hope is not the denial of pain; it is confidence in Jesus's completion of all that He promised.
Humanity has always asked whether brokenness will have the final word. The new heaven and the new earth answer without hesitation: no. God does.

KEY SCRIPTURES

Please read the scriptures, then answer the questions that follow.

ONE

REVELATION 21:1–4 NIV

"Then I saw 'a new heaven and a new earth,' for the first heaven and the first earth had passed away, and there was no longer any sea. I saw the Holy City, the new Jerusalem, coming down out of heaven from God, prepared as a bride beautifully dressed for her husband. And I heard a loud voice from the throne saying, 'Look! God's dwelling place is now among the people, and he will dwell with them. They will be his people, and God himself will be with them and be their God. He will wipe every tear from their eyes. There will be no more death or mourning or crying or pain, for the old order of things has passed away.'"

TWO

ISAIAH 65:17–19 NIV

"See, I will create new heavens and a new earth. The former things will not be remembered, nor will they come to mind. But be glad and rejoice forever in what I will create, for I will create Jerusalem to be a delight and its people a joy. I will rejoice over Jerusalem and take delight in my people; the sound of weeping and of crying will be heard in it no more."

THREE

JOHN 14:1–3 NIV

"Do not let your hearts be troubled. You believe in God; believe also in me. My Father's house has many rooms; if that were not so, would I have told you that I am going there to prepare a place for you? And if I go and prepare a place for you, I will come back and take you to be with me that you also may be where I am."

FOUR

2 PETER 3:10–13 NIV

"But the day of the Lord will come like a thief. The heavens will disappear with a roar; the elements will be destroyed by fire, and the earth and everything done in it will be laid bare. Since everything will be destroyed in this way, what kind of people ought you to be? You ought to live holy and godly lives as you look forward to the day of God and speed its coming. That day will bring about the destruction of the heavens by fire, and the elements will melt in the heat. But in keeping with his promise we are looking forward to a new heaven and a new earth, where righteousness dwells."

191

NEXT

KEY SCRIPTURES

Please read the scriptures, then answer the questions that follow.

REVELATION 21:5-8 NIV

ONE

"He who was seated on the throne said, 'I am making everything new!' Then he said, 'Write this down, for these words are trustworthy and true.' He said to me: 'It is done. I am the Alpha and the Omega, the Beginning and the End. To the thirsty I will give water without cost from the spring of the water of life. Those who are victorious will inherit all this, and I will be their God and they will be my children. But the cowardly, the unbelieving, the vile, the murderers, the sexually immoral, those who practice magic arts, the idolaters and all liars—they will be consigned to the fiery lake of burning sulfur. This is the second death.'"

REVELATION 22:1-5 NIV

TWO

"Then the angel showed me the river of the water of life, as clear as crystal, flowing from the throne of God and of the Lamb down the middle of the great street of the city. On each side of the river stood the tree of life, bearing twelve crops of fruit, yielding its fruit every month. And the leaves of the tree are for the healing of the nations. No longer will there be any curse. The throne of God and of the Lamb will be in the city, and his servants will serve him. They will see his face, and his name will be on their foreheads. There will be no more night. They will not need the light of a lamp or the light of the sun, for the Lord God will give them light. And they will reign for ever and ever."

ISAIAH 66:22-24 NIV

THREE

"'As the new heavens and the new earth that I make will endure before me,' declares the Lord, 'so will your name and descendants endure. From one New Moon to another and from one Sabbath to another, all mankind will come and bow down before me,' says the Lord. 'And they will go out and look on the dead bodies of those who rebelled against me; the worms that eat them will not die, the fire that burns them will not be quenched, and they will be loathsome to all mankind.'"

192

GROUP DISCUSSION QUESTIONS

CONSIDER THE SCRIPTURES READ, THEN ANSWER THE FOLLOWING QUESTIONS.

How does understanding eternity as restoration change common ideas about heaven?

1

Why is it important that identity is preserved rather than erased in resurrection?

2

What does the absence of the sea reveal about God's vision for peace?

3

How should belief in a new heaven and a new earth shape how believers live now?

4

NEXT

Prayer

Father God,

Forgive us for knowing so much and discerning so little.
Cleanse us from complacency and distraction.
Give us eyes to see the seasons,
ears to hear Your warnings,
and hearts willing to align without delay.
Teach us to recognize mercy in Your patience
and urgency in Your silence.
Keep our lamps filled, our love pure,
and our obedience ready.
We refuse sleep that dulls our awareness.
We reject compromise and choose faithfulness.
We declare that we will not be surprised or fearful.
We will be found watching and ready.
In the name of Jesus our Lord we pray,
Amen.

CHAPTER 22 NEW JERUSALEM – THE BRIDE OF THE LAMB

NEXT

"I saw the Holy City, the new Jerusalem, coming down out of heaven from God, prepared as a bride beautifully dressed for her husband."

—Revelation 21:2 NIV

The final image John gives us is not a city made of stone. It is a people made ready. John does not see humanity escaping upward into heaven. He sees heaven descending down to earth. This distinction of the direction matters. God does not remove His redeemed creation forever; He comes to dwell with it fully. What began in Eden with God walking among humanity ends with God establishing His dwelling permanently in their midst.

The city is called a bride because the end of history is not conquest alone—it is union. From the beginning, God sought relationship, not distance. He did not rescue humanity merely to rule over them, but to dwell with them. The language of bride tells us that the covenant is fulfilled, love is consummated, and the separation is over. Redemption reaches its most intimate and triumphant expression. What was promised is not merely delivered—it is embraced.

This Bride is not improvised or rushed but she is prepared. Her beauty is the result of endurance, faithfulness, and allegiance refined across generations. She has been purified through suffering, shaped by obedience, and marked by loyalty to the Lamb. Nothing in this moment is accidental or hurried. What endured through persecution, trial, and hope now shines with glory.

NEXT

NEW JERUSALEM – THE BRIDE OF THE LAMB

"I saw the Holy City, the new Jerusalem, coming down out of heaven from God, prepared as a bride beautifully dressed for her husband."
—Revelation 21:2

John tells us the city has no need of sun or moon, because the glory of God gives it light, and the Lamb is its lamp. God's presence is no longer mediated through symbols, shadows, or structures. There is no dimness because there is no distance. Darkness has no refuge here. Light is not created—it is embodied.

The gates of the city are never shut. This means peace replaces vulnerability. Nothing and no one can threaten, invade, or corrupt here. Security will not depend on walls or vigilance, but on righteousness fully established. That is because fear has no function where holiness reigns.

John then sees something astonishing: the nations are healed. *"Then the angel showed me the river of the water of life, as clear as crystal, flowing from the throne of God and of the Lamb down the middle of the great street of the city. On each side of the river stood the tree of life, bearing twelve crops of fruit, yielding its fruit every month. And the leaves of the tree are for the healing of the nations.*

No longer will there be any curse. The throne of God and of the Lamb will be in the city, and his servants will serve him." [Rev. 22:1-3 NIV]

The leaves of the tree of life are for their healing. The wounds of peoples, cultures, and civilizations are not dismissed or forgotten. They are healed. Justice does not end with judgment; it continues with restoration. What sin fractured across centuries is mended in the presence of God.

John notes with awe that there is no temple in the city. This is the final answer to every sacred longing. No building or ritual remains. There are no more mediators standing between. God and the Lamb are the dwelling place. What was once approached carefully is now inhabited freely. Worship is no longer a destination—it is the atmosphere of existence.

Revelation 22:3 declares that the curse is gone. The curse introduced in Eden is fully undone. Labor exists without frustration. Authority is

NEXT

NEW JERUSALEM – THE BRIDE OF THE LAMB

exercised without corruption. Love is lived without fear. Life continues without death. The long arc of Scripture, from Genesis to Revelation, completes its journey. Nothing remains unresolved.

God's people are not passive residents in this city, either. They reign forever and ever. This reign is about stewardship and not domination. Humanity finally fulfills its original calling: to rule with God, under God, in harmony with creation. What Adam lost is restored beyond loss.

The Bible does not end with humanity climbing to God through effort or escape. It ends with God coming to humanity in love. Justice moves toward restoration. Faith moves toward sight. Hope becomes reality and love reaches union.

Every longing of the human heart—belonging, safety, purpose, and love—is answered here. The Bride of the Lamb declares the final truth of history: You were made for communion with God, and that communion is now complete.

"Jesus replied, 'Anyone who loves me will obey my teaching. My Father will love them, and we will come to them and make our home with them.'"
~John 14:23 NIV

NEXT

KEY SCRIPTURES

Please read the scriptures, then answer the questions that follow.

REVELATION 21:2-5 NIV

"I saw the Holy City, the new Jerusalem, coming down out of heaven from God, prepared as a bride beautifully dressed for her husband. And I heard a loud voice from the throne saying, 'Look! God's dwelling place is now among the people, and he will dwell with them. They will be his people, and God himself will be with them and be their God. He will wipe every tear from their eyes. There will be no more death or mourning or crying or pain, for the old order of things has passed away.'"

ONE

HEBREWS 11:10, 16 NIV

"For he was looking forward to the city with foundations, whose architect and builder is God. Instead, they were longing for a better country—a heavenly one. Therefore God is not ashamed to be called their God, for he has prepared a city for them."

TWO

JOHN 14:23 NIV

"Jesus replied, 'Anyone who loves me will obey my teaching. My Father will love them, and we will come to them and make our home with them.'"

THREE

ISAIAH 62:1-5 NIV

"For Zion's sake I will not keep silent, for Jerusalem's sake I will not remain quiet, till her vindication shines out like the dawn, her salvation like a blazing torch. The nations will see your vindication, and all kings your glory; you will be called by a new name that the mouth of the Lord will bestow. You will be a crown of splendor in the Lord's hand, a royal diadem in the hand of your God. No longer will they call you Deserted, or name your land Desolate. But you will be called Hephzibah, and your land Beulah; for the Lord will take delight in you, and your land will be married. As a young man marries a young woman, so will your Builder marry you; as a bridegroom rejoices over his bride, so will your God rejoice over you."

FOUR

NEXT

KEY SCRIPTURES

Please read the scripture, then answer the questions that follow.

REVELATION 21: 9–27 NIV

"One of the seven angels who had the seven bowls full of the seven last plagues came and said to me, 'Come, I will show you the bride, the wife of the Lamb.' And he carried me away in the Spirit to a mountain great and high, and showed me the Holy City, Jerusalem, coming down out of heaven from God. It shone with the glory of God, and its brilliance was like that of a very precious jewel, like a jasper, clear as crystal. It had a great, high wall with twelve gates, and with twelve angels at the gates. On the gates were written the names of the twelve tribes of Israel. There were three gates on the east, three on the north, three on the south and three on the west. The wall of the city had twelve foundations, and on them were the names of the twelve apostles of the Lamb. The angel who talked with me had a measuring rod of gold to measure the city, its gates and its walls. The city was laid out like a square, as long as it was wide. He measured the city with the rod and found it to be 12,000 stadia in length, and as wide and high as it is long The angel measured the wall using human measurement, and it was 144 cubits thick. The wall was made of jasper, and the city of pure gold, as pure as glass. The foundations of the city walls were decorated with every kind of precious stone. The first foundation was jasper, the second sapphire, the third agate, the fourth emerald, the fifth onyx, the sixth ruby, the seventh chrysolite, the eighth beryl, the ninth topaz, the tenth turquoise, the eleventh jacinth, and the twelfth amethyst. The twelve gates were twelve pearls, each gate made of a single pearl. The great street of the city was of gold, as pure as transparent glass. I did not see a temple in the city, because the Lord God Almighty and the Lamb are its temple. The city does not need the sun or the moon to shine on it, for the glory of God gives it light, and the Lamb is its lamp. The nations will walk by its light, and the kings of the earth will bring their splendor into it. On no day will its gates ever be shut, for there will be no night there. The glory and honor of the nations will be brought into it. Nothing impure will ever enter it, nor will anyone who does what is shameful or deceitful, but only those whose names are written in the Lamb's book of life."

NEXT

KEY SCRIPTURES

Please read the scriptures, then answer the questions that follow.

REVELATION 22:1–5 NIV

"Then the angel showed me the river of the water of life, as clear as crystal, flowing from the throne of God and of the Lamb down the middle of the great street of the city. On each side of the river stood the tree of life, bearing twelve crops of fruit, yielding its fruit every month. And the leaves of the tree are for the healing of the nations. No longer will there be any curse. The throne of God and of the Lamb will be in the city, and his servants will serve him. They will see his face, and his name will be on their foreheads. There will be no more night. They will not need the light of a lamp or the light of the sun, for the Lord God will give them light. And they will reign for ever and ever."

GROUP DISCUSSION QUESTIONS

CONSIDER THE SCRIPTURES READ, THEN ANSWER THE FOLLOWING QUESTIONS.

Why does Scripture end with heaven descending rather than humanity ascending?

1

What does it mean that the New Jerusalem is described as a Bride rather than merely a city?

2

How does the healing of the nations reshape our understanding of eternity?

3

What does reigning with God look like when domination and corruption are removed?

4

203

NEXT

Prayer

Faithful Bridegroom and Eternal King,
You did not redeem us to keep us at a distance,
but to dwell with us forever. Prepare our hearts
with faithfulness, our lives with holiness,
and our hope with confidence in Your promises.
Heal what history has wounded. Restore what sin
has broken.
Teach us to live now as citizens of the City that
is coming.
We long not merely for heaven—we long for You.
And we rejoice that You are coming to dwell
with us.
Make us ready. Make us faithful. Make us Yours
forever.
In Your name we pray,
Amen.

CHAPTER 23
THE TEMPLE, THE RED HEIFER, & OTHER SACRED QUESTIONS

NEXT

"For Zion's sake I will not keep silent, for Jerusalem's sake I will not remain quiet, till her vindication shines out like the dawn, her salvation like a blazing torch. The nations will see your vindication, and all kings your glory; you will be called by a new name that the mouth of the Lord will bestow. You will be a crown of splendor in the Lord's hand, a royal diadem in the hand of your God. No longer will they call you Deserted, or name your land Desolate. But you will be called Hephzibah, and your land Beulah; for the Lord will take delight in you, and your land will be married. As a young man marries a young woman, so will your Builder marry you; as a bridegroom rejoices over his bride, so will your God rejoice over you."

— ISAIAH 62:1–5 NIV

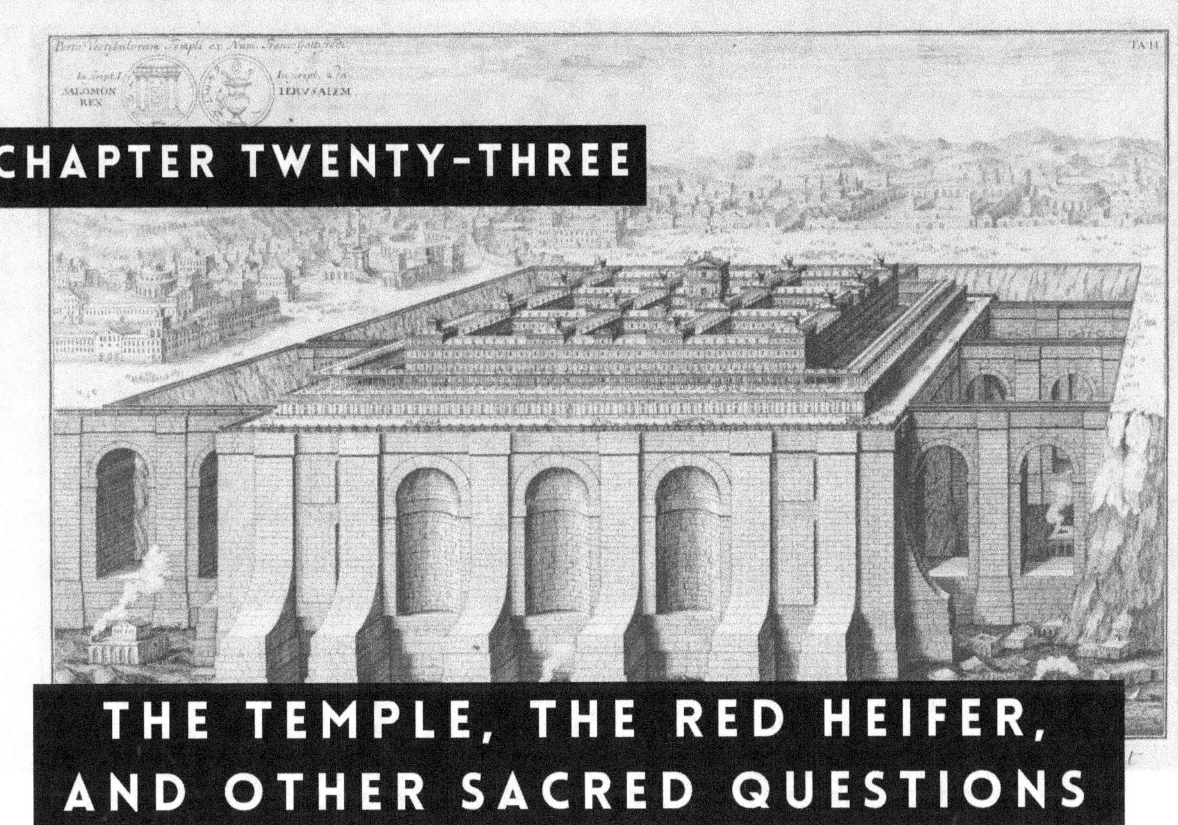

THE TEMPLE, THE RED HEIFER, AND OTHER SACRED QUESTIONS

For the Jews, few subjects stir their souls more than the rebuilding of the Temple, the restoration of sacrifice, and the mystery of the red heifer. This is more than just curiosities. These details touch on covenant, worship, identity, atonement, and the hope of the Messiah. They are questions that reach backward into Sinai and forward into the end of the age. But they must be handled with clarity that comes from prophetic Scriptures, not speculative fascination.

The Temple in biblical history was never merely stone and cedar. When God's glory filled it in 1 Kings 8, it declared that the Holy One chooses to dwell among His covenant people. When it fell in 2 Kings 25, it testified that sacrifice of animals cannot substitute for obedience. Rituals without obedience invites God's judgment. The Temple was the meeting place of heaven and earth, the center of sacrifice, and the axis of national identity, but the Temple always pointed forward to something greater.

The prophet Ezekiel exiled and grieving, in chapters 40–48 was carried by the Spirit to encounter a future Temple in meticulous architectural detail. Zechariah 6:12–13 speaks of "the Branch" who will build the Temple of the Lord. Isaiah 2:2–3 envisions nations streaming to the mountain of the Lord. In traditional Jewish expectation,

NEXT

THE TEMPLE, THE RED HEIFER, AND OTHER SACRED QUESTIONS

"Do you not know that you yourselves are God's temple and that God's Spirit dwells in your midst?"
— 1 Corinthians 3:16 NIV

these passages are not symbolic abstractions. They are promises. They believe that the Messiah will rebuild the Temple, Jerusalem will become the center of global worship, and sacrificial service will resume.

Religious tradition strengthens this expectation. The medieval scholar Maimonides taught that the Messiah will rebuild the Temple and gather the dispersed of Israel.[1] In mainstream Orthodox Judaism, Temple restoration is not optional; it is a mark of Messianic legitimacy.

This is not trivial but covenantal. And yet, when Jesus stood in Jerusalem and declared, *"Destroy this temple, and I will raise it again in three days,"* [John 2:19 NIV] Scripture clarifies that He was speaking of His body. [Hebrews 10:10] He did not diminish the Temple; He embodied it. The dwelling place of God was no longer confined to geography. It stood before them in flesh and blood.

The writer of Hebrews speaks with blazing clarity: "We have been made holy through the sacrifice of the body of Jesus Christ once and for all." [Hebrews 10:10 NIV] And again: "The blood of bulls and goats cannot take away sins." *[Hebrews 10:4 CEV]* Under the New Covenant, sacrifice is complete, atonement is finished, and the veil is torn.

The question shifts from "Where is the Temple?" to "Who is the Temple?" This is where the debate intensifies. Passages like Daniel 9:27; Jesus's reference to the abomination that causes desolation in Matthew 24:15, and Paul's warning in 2 Thessalonians 2:4 about one who exalts himself in God's temple suggest a future focal point of desecration. Scripture allows for sober discussion of this future event. It may involve a restored structure or a visible religious authority, but nowhere does the New Covenant teach that sacrifices must resume. Architecture may rise, rituals may be rehearsed, but no altar built by human hands can improve upon Calvary.

Yet Ezekiel 39 reminds us that God's

[1] MAIMONIDES - LAWS PERTAINING TO THE MESSIAH. JEWS FOR JUDAISM. (2014, FEBRUARY 6).
HTTPS://JEWSFORJUDAISM.ORG/KNOWLEDGE/ARTICLES/MAIMONIDES-LAWS-PERTAINING-MESSIAH

NEXT

THE TEMPLE, THE RED HEIFER, AND OTHER SACRED QUESTIONS

restoration for the Israelites is not over. He made an everlasting covenant with Israel and He will finish what He began. After Gog's defeat, God will gather Israel fully and pour out His Spirit on them. It is that same Spirit poured out at Pentecost on the early believers at the beginning of the Church who will seal the promise of full reconciliation. Therefore, the bride of Christ and the chosen people are not rivals in prophecy. They converge in the Messiah who is Jesus the Christ. The cross accomplished what bulls, rams, and goats never could. The veil is torn, access is opened, and the Spirit now indwells in temples not made by hands.

But there's still the question of the red heifer. In Numbers 19, the red heifer was required for ritual purification. It had to be without blemish. Its ashes cleansed defilement that came from contact with a human corpse so that worship could proceed. It was rare, specific, and sacred. Today, renewed interest in breeding a flawless red heifer reflects longing for restoration of the Temple, legitimacy of their claims, and preparation for what has already taken place through the finished work of the Cross.

But Hebrews 10:1 stands unshaken: The sacrificial system was a shadow of the substance of what Christ fulfilled when He was raised from the dead. The red heifer pointed toward cleansing, but the Cross accomplished it, and the Spirit applies it internally for those who receive Jesus as Savior. The ash from the red heifer purified the flesh; Jesus's Blood cleanses the conscience, and the Spirit transforms the heart. Purification is no longer ash applied externally but Jesus's blood applied eternally. Therefore, cleansing is no longer a ritual to be repeated but the completion of covenant.

These questions become dangerous when they replace obedience with speculation. Paul warns not to be captivated by shadows, for the reality found only in Christ. *"Do not let anyone judge you by what you eat or drink… These are a shadow of the things that were to come; the reality, however, is found in Christ."* [Colossians 2:16–17 NIV] Shadows are meaningful—but they are not the substance of our faith.

Why does God allow such debate to linger? Because it reveals where faith is anchored. Judaism awaits a Messiah who will validate Himself by rebuilding the Temple. Christianity confesses that the Messiah already validated Himself by becoming the Temple and offering Himself once for all.

NEXT

THE TEMPLE, THE RED HEIFER, AND OTHER SACRED QUESTIONS

This is not a minor divergence. It is a defining one. For Judaism, the sequence is often understood as: When the Messiah comes, the Temple will be rebuilt. For us—those who believe in Jesus as the Christ confess that the Messiah has already come in the person of Jesus Christ and He fulfills the sanctification that sacrifices for the Jews and the original Temple could only temporarily cleanse.

And John, in Revelation, gives the final word. *"I did not see a temple in the city, because the Lord God Almighty and the Lamb are its temple."* [Rev. 21:22 NIV] The end of the story is not a restored building. It is never-ending presence of our Savior. There will be no veil, altar, or barrier. God Himself and Jesus, the Lamb, will dwell fully with His people.

So beneath every debate about blueprints and ashes burns one sacred question: Is Christ enough? If He is, then no rebuilt Temple can add to Him, no resumed ritual can complete Him, and every prophecy is fulfilled in Him. The Temple was the promise; the red heifer was a shadow; the Messiah is the fulfillment, and Jesus Christ stands at the center of them all.

"Do not let your hearts be troubled. You believe in God; believe also in me."
~ John 14:1 NIV

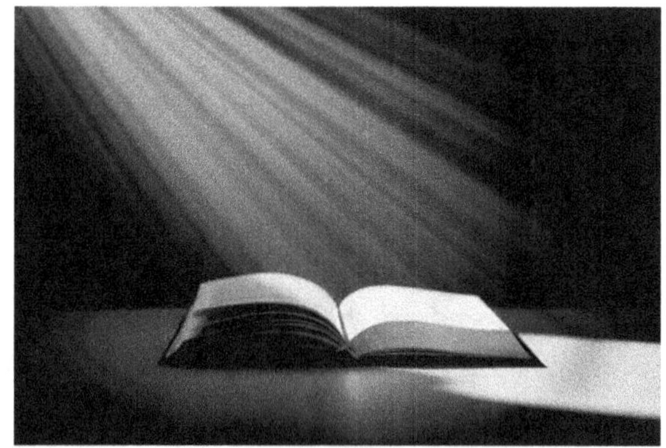

NEXT

KEY SCRIPTURES

Please read the scriptures, then answer the questions that follow.

ONE

HEBREWS 10:1 NIV

"The law is only a shadow of the good things that are coming—not the realities themselves. For this reason it can never, by the same sacrifices repeated endlessly year after year, make perfect those who draw near to worship."

TWO

ZECHARIAH 6:12–13 NIV

"Tell him this is what the Lord Almighty says: 'Here is the man whose name is the Branch, and he will branch out from his place and build the temple of the Lord. It is he who will build the temple of the Lord, and he will be clothed with majesty and will sit and rule on his throne. And he will be a priest on his throne. And there will be harmony between the two.'"

THREE

ISAIAH 2:2–3 NIV

"In the last days the mountain of the Lord's temple will be established as the highest of the mountains; it will be exalted above the hills, and all nations will stream to it. Many peoples will come and say, 'Come, let us go up to the mountain of the Lord, to the temple of the God of Jacob. He will teach us his ways, so that we may walk in his paths.' The law will go out from Zion, the word of the Lord from Jerusalem."

FOUR

JOHN 2:19–21 NIV

"Jesus answered them, 'Destroy this temple, and I will raise it again in three days.' They replied, 'It has taken forty-six years to build this temple, and you are going to raise it in three days?' But the temple he had spoken of was his body."

FIVE

HEBREWS 10:4,10 NIV

"It is impossible for the blood of bulls and goats to take away sins. And by that will, we have been made holy through the sacrifice of the body of Jesus Christ once for all."

NEXT

KEY SCRIPTURES

Please read the scriptures, then answer the questions that follow.

ONE

COLOSSIANS 2:16–17 NIV

"Therefore do not let anyone judge you by what you eat or drink, or with regard to a religious festival, a New Moon celebration or a Sabbath day. These are a shadow of the things that were to come; the reality, however, is found in Christ."

TWO

REVELATION 21:22 NIV

"I did not see a temple in the city, because the Lord God Almighty and the Lamb are its temple."

THREE

REVELATION 14:1 NIV

"Then I looked, and there before me was the Lamb, standing on Mount Zion, and with him 144,000 who had his name and his Father's name written on their foreheads."

FOUR

HEBREWS 12:22–24 NIV

"But you have come to Mount Zion, to the city of the living God, the heavenly Jerusalem. You have come to thousands upon thousands of angels in joyful assembly, to the church of the firstborn, whose names are written in heaven. You have come to God, the Judge of all, to the spirits of the righteous made perfect, to Jesus the mediator of a new covenant, and to the sprinkled blood that speaks a better word than the blood of Abel."

FIVE

ROMANS 11:26–29 NIV

"And in this way all Israel will be saved. As it is written: 'The deliverer will come from Zion; he will turn godlessness away from Jacob. And this is my covenant with them when I take away their sins.' As far as the gospel is concerned, they are enemies for your sake; but as far as election is concerned, they are loved on account of the patriarchs, for God's gifts and his call are irrevocable."

NEXT

GROUP DISCUSSION QUESTIONS

CONSIDER THE SCRIPTURES READ, THEN ANSWER THE FOLLOWING QUESTIONS.

ONE — Why is the Temple central in both Jewish and Christian theology?

TWO — How do Ezekiel's and Zechariah's prophecies shape Jewish Messianic expectation?

THREE — How does John 2 redefine sacred space?

FOUR — What does Hebrews 10 settle about sacrifice?

FIVE — How should believers approach debates about a future Temple?

SIX — What dangers arise from prophetic obsession?

SEVEN — Is Christ sufficient in your theology—or do you unconsciously add to Him?

213

Prayer

Holy God,
You who filled the Temple with glory and tore the veil with mercy, keep us anchored in what is finished. Guard us from fascination that eclipses faith in the finished work of Jesus, **the Promised Messiah.** Protect us from systems that rival Your Son. Fix our eyes on Christ—the true Temple, the final sacrifice, and the dwelling place of God with humanity. May we be found faithful, not fascinated; anchored, not alarmed; steadfast in the Lamb who fulfills every promise. In the holy name of Jesus we pray, **Amen.**

CHAPTER 24
WHAT'S NEXT?

"Then I heard another voice from heaven saying, 'Come out of her, my people, lest you share in her sins, and lest you receive of her plagues.'" — Revelation 18:4

You have come to the close of this book, with all of the words of Jesus mapped out for our understanding. But all of this begs the question: Now that we're here, what do we do with this? We must understand the times and the seasons without trepidation. We must press forward knowing that our vindication is coming soon. But we also must understand the clear instructions outlined in this scripture: "Come out of her."

As the book of Revelation approaches its climax, the apostle John is shown a striking vision of a woman who represents a powerful and corrupt system operating in the world. She is described as clothed in purple and scarlet, adorned with gold, precious stones, and pearls, and holding a golden cup filled with abominations. She rides upon the beast, symbolizing a close alliance between religious influence and political power. The imagery is vivid and deliberate. This woman is not presented as a single individual but as a symbolic representation of a vast system that exerts influence over nations, rulers, economies, and cultures.

NEXT

WHAT NEXT?

Scripture identifies her as "Babylon the Great, the Mother of Prostitutes and of the Abominations of the Earth." [Rev. 17:5] The name Babylon carries deep historical significance throughout the Bible. In the Old Testament, Babylon was the empire that conquered Jerusalem and carried Israel into exile. It became a symbol of rebellion against God, arrogance, idolatry, and oppressive power. In Revelation, the name is used again to describe a global system that embodies similar characteristics—wealth, influence, spiritual corruption, and opposition to God's truth.

John is told that the woman represents "the great city that rules over the kings of the earth." [Rev. 17:18] This statement emphasizes that the system symbolized by Babylon possesses extraordinary influence over political authority. Kings are depicted as committing adultery with her, which suggests an unholy partnership between worldly power and spiritual corruption. Throughout history, political rulers have often aligned themselves with religious leaders in order to consolidate power, legitimize rule,

and control populations. When spiritual authority becomes entangled with the pursuit of political dominance, the result is frequently distortion of truth and abuse of power.

Revelation also records a sobering observation about this woman: she is "drunk with the blood of the saints and with the blood of the witnesses of Jesus." [Rev. 17:6] This language reflects the persecution that believers have endured across centuries. Faithful followers of Christ have often suffered not only under secular regimes but also under religious systems that sought to silence dissent and maintain institutional control. Whenever authority persecutes those who remain loyal to the Word of God, the spirit of Babylon is revealed.

Yet Babylon's power does not operate through force alone. Revelation portrays her influence as seductive. Kings and merchants alike are drawn to her wealth, luxury, and promise of prosperity. The merchants of the earth grow rich through her commerce, and the nations

WHAT'S NEXT?

become intoxicated with her influence. This imagery points to the powerful attraction of systems that promise economic security, prestige, and cultural dominance while quietly leading people away from faithfulness to God.

For us, who believe in Jesus, the greatest danger is often not persecution but assimilation. Systems like Babylon do not always demand immediate rebellion against God; instead, they encourage compromise. They invite believers to adjust their convictions, soften their allegiance to truth, and blend into the surrounding culture. Over time, compromise erodes faithfulness.

It is in this context that heaven issues a direct command: "Come out of her, my people." [Rev. 18:4] This instruction is not simply a call to leave a geographical location or withdraw from society. Rather, it is a call to spiritual separation. God calls us to refuse participation in corruption, deception, and systems that replace obedience to Him with loyalty to worldly power.

This theme of separation appears repeatedly throughout Scripture. Abraham was called to leave his homeland and follow God into the unknown. Israel was delivered from Egypt so that they could become a distinct people devoted to the Lord. The early church was called to turn away from idolatry and live differently from the surrounding culture. In every era, God's people are called to remain distinct in their loyalty and obedience.

Revelation also reveals that Babylon's apparent strength is temporary. Although she appears powerful and secure, her fall comes suddenly. The kings who once aligned themselves with her will eventually turn against her, and her system will collapse under divine judgment. The merchants and rulers of the earth mourn her destruction because their wealth and power were tied to her prosperity. What once appeared permanent proves fragile when confronted with the justice of God.

The final chapters of Revelation contrast Babylon with another woman—the Bride, described as the New Jerusalem coming down from heaven, prepared as a bride adorned for her husband. These two images represent two fundamentally different allegiances. Babylon symbolizes corruption, compromise, and rebellion against God, while the Bride represents purity, faithfulness, and covenant relationship with Jesus Christ.

WHAT'S NEXT?

Every generation faces the same choice between these two allegiances. Babylon appeals to power, wealth, and influence in the present world. The Bride represents loyalty to Jesus Christ and participation in the kingdom that will endure forever. Revelation makes clear that the systems of Babylon will ultimately fall, while the kingdom of God will stand forever.

Understanding these prophetic visions is not meant to produce fear or speculation. Instead, prophecy serves to cultivate discernment and faithfulness among believers. The purpose of Revelation is not merely to describe future events but to encourage the people of God to remain steadfast in their devotion to Christ regardless of the pressures around them.

The book concludes with the assurance that every counterfeit system will eventually collapse. Babylon will fall, the beast will be destroyed, and death itself will be defeated. Ultimately, *"the kingdom of the world has become the kingdom of our Lord and of His Messiah, and He will reign forever and ever."* [Rev. 11:22]

The final message of Revelation is therefore both a warning and an invitation. The warning is that religious systems built on deception and compromise cannot endure. The invitation is that God calls us, His people, to belong to a different kingdom—one defined not by worldly power but by righteousness, truth, and faithfulness to Jesus, the Christ.

For those who read these words, the question is not simply how Babylon will fall. Scripture has already declared that outcome. The deeper question is whether God's people will recognize the systems that oppose Him and respond to His call to come out from them.

The final voice of Scripture echoes with invitation: *"The Spirit and the bride say, 'Come.'"* [Rev. 21:22] Those who hear this call are invited to remain faithful to Jesus and to place their hope not in the temporary structures of this world, but in the eternal kingdom that He will establish.

NEXT

1 — CLARIFY THE MESSAGE
Know the Gospel of the Kingdom, not substitutes.

2 — DISCERN THE MOMENT
Recognize urgency without panic.

3 — SPEAK TRUTH FAITHFULLY
Share Christ with truth, humility, and courage.

4 — SUPPORT THE MISSION
Pray, give, send, and strengthen those who go.

5 — REFUSE SILENCE
Bear witness in word, life, and allegiance. Keep eternal perspective without neglecting present obedience.

6 — PRAY REGULARLY
Pray for unreached nations and persecuted believers.

7 — USE AVAILABLE TOOLS
Use technology, your voice, and/or presence —to testify faithfully.

NOTES

YOUR

FEEDBACK

IS IMPORTANT TO US

Did you enjoy this course/ebook?

☺ We loved it! ☹ As expected ☹

How would you rate your instructor? 1 2 3 4 5

What did you most like about this course/ebook?

____

____

How likely are you to recommend us to your family & friends?

unlikely **0 1 2 3 4 5 6 7 8 9 10** Definitely !

How would you rate the content and course materials?

Poor   Fair   Acceptable   Good   Excellent

If you have any other comments or suggestions, we would love to hear them below!

THANK YOU FOR YOUR FEEDBACK!

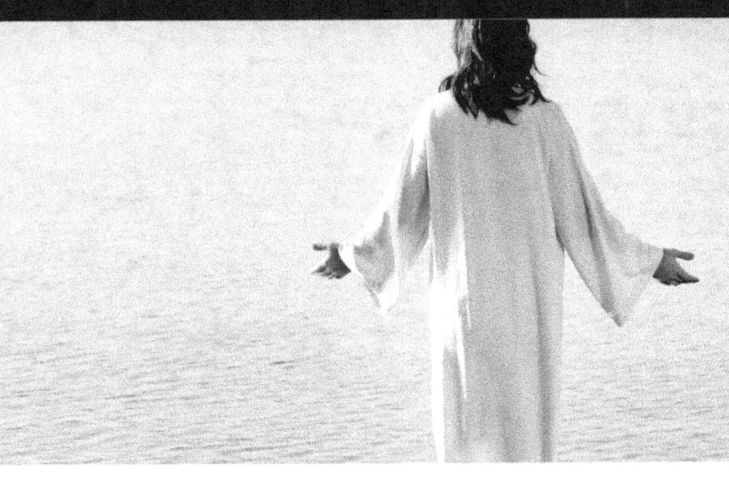

JOIN THE MOVEMENT!

AND BECOME A PART OF THE TRIBE TODAY!

We're building a community of believers that stand on the word of God that says we are a chosen generation that will perform the greater works that Jesus said that we would. If you agree with this mission, please consider joining our community as we connect our faith for the impossible to become possible. We look forward to seeing you at other courses, either on Zoom or live and in person at our retreats and other events. Stay tuned.

MIRACLE MOVEMENT

MIRACLE-MOVEMENT.COM

I-AM-SALT.COM

BOOKS WRITTEN BY LAURAINE WHITE

Chosen

Originally published in 2016, Lauraine White pushes the bar while telling much of her life's story. She tells of how God opened a door for her to witness, first hand, the inner workings of international ministries in order for her to see the new age of idol worship. It was and always will be an abomination.

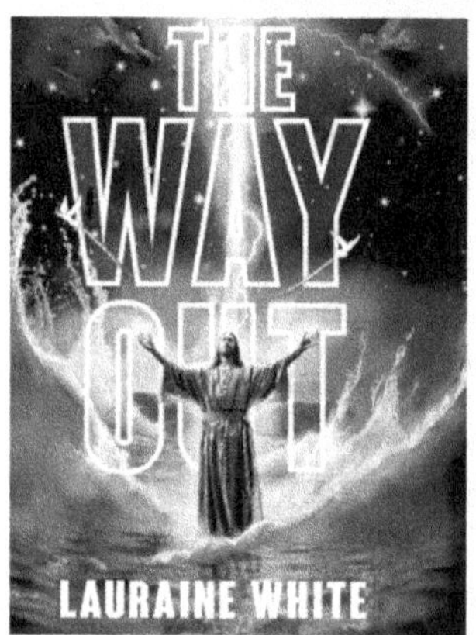

The Way Out

After some very traumatic events in her life, Lauraine White, needed a way out. This story, inspired by those events, is told along with how she got out. The message is simple and clear. Jesus is our only way out.

Bulletproof

Inspired by a dream, Lauraine White delivers a call to action message to the Church to come back to its first love and do the work that it is called to do, especially in times like these when many have fallen away from the Truth.

MASTER CLASSES OFFERED

THE WAY OUT MASTER CLASS

Prepare to embark on a journey of discovery. You are here by divine design and being called to God's Army. This call requires that you be equipped with not just any weapons but by those that make demons quiver.

In this workbook, Lauraine shares exercises that will push you to prepare a workable life plan. The work you will do will launch you into your destiny. You will laugh, cry, and realize that you are meant for so much more than what you thought. God's original plans for your life begins now.

BULLETPROOF MASTER CLASS

A prolific writer and speaker, Lauraine White comes with a bold project-Bulletproof Master Class to educate and equip believers in Jesus Christ. These lessons enlighten students on how to overcome the battles brought on by our adversary, Satan. Through bible study and practical exercises, Lauraine leads her students to understand the keys of the Kingdom of Heaven that gives us authority over all the powers of Satan. When this is understood, dominion on earth can be realized. These processes are tried and true methods she used, under the direction of the Holy Spirits to find her own way out of some very dark places. Prepare to be challenged and motivated to see Jesus in a whole new way. He's worth a second look.

LEAVE US A
REVIEW

We hope you enjoyed our Master Class and found lots of value to help you! We would appreciate if you wouldn't mind taking the time to leave us a review. Thanks!

Lauraine White

THANK YOU FOR YOUR FEEDBACK!

COPYRIGHT NOTICE

CONTACT US FOR MORE INFORMATION

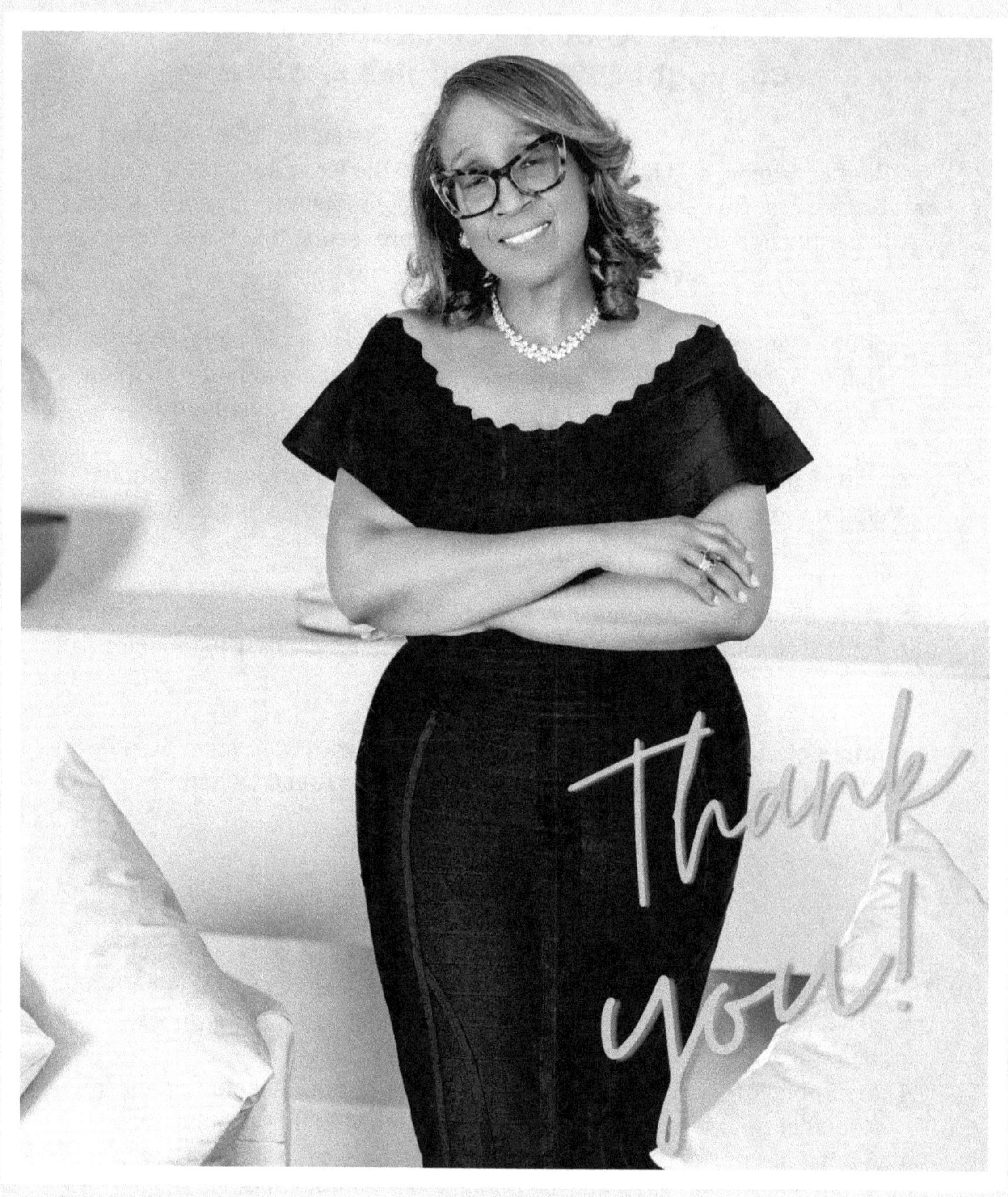

NEXT

BY LAURAINE WHITE

www.ingramcontent.com/pod-product-compliance
Lightning Source LLC
Chambersburg PA
CBHW081925120726
47997CB00010B/3044